Everyday Early Learning

Other Redleaf Books by Jeff A. Johnson

*Finding Your Smile Again: A Child Care Professional's Guide
to Reducing Stress and Avoiding Burnout*

*Do-It-Yourself Early Learning: Easy and Fun Activities
and Toys from Everyday Home Center Materials*
(with Tasha A. Johnson)

Everyday
Early Learning

Easy and Fun Activities and Toys
from Stuff You Can Find Around the House

Jeff A. Johnson

with Zoë Johnson

Redleaf Press®
www.redleafpress.org
800-423-8309

Published by Redleaf Press
10 Yorkton Court
St. Paul, MN 55117
www.redleafpress.org

First edition 2008
Cover design by Percolator
Cover photographs by Jeff A. Johnson
Interior typeset in ITC Stone Informal and designed by Percolator
Interior photographs by Jeff A. Johnson
Interior illustrations by Chris Wold Dyrud
Printed in the United States of America

18 17 16 15 14 13 12 11   3 4 5 6 7 8 9 10

Library of Congress Cataloging-in-Publication Data
Johnson, Jeff A., 1969–
    Everyday early learning : easy and fun activities and toys from stuff you can find around the house /
Jeff A. Johnson with Zoë Johnson. — 1st ed.
       p. cm.
    ISBN 978-1-933653-42-6 (alk. paper)
    1. Early childhood education—Activity programs. I. Johnson, Zoë. II. Title.
LB1139.35.A37J635 2008
372.21—dc22
                                                                                          2007046219

Printed on acid-free paper

To my mom, for always being there for me and putting up with me all these years. —JJ

To my mom, for always being there for me and putting up with me all these years. —ZJ

Real learning is a process of discovery, and if we want it to happen, we must create the kinds of conditions in which discoveries are made. We know what these are. They include time, leisure, freedom, and lack of pressure.

—John Holt, *Learning All the Time*

Everyday Early Learning

Acknowledgments

First off, I would like to thank Tasha Johnson for being such an awesome wife and mom. She contributed a lot of ideas to this book and put up with a lot of messes around the house as Zoë and I developed projects.

I would like to thank Hunter, Jack, Sam, Maddie, Ty, Phoebe, Siddha, Marygrace, Noah, Kia, RJ, Madison, Jordan, Ethan, Jadyn, Jaden, Brenden, and Adrian, who helped test out the following projects and activities in our family child care program over the last few years. I would like to also thank the children who tried things out on our visits to their child care programs.

Special thanks to the following people and programs for letting us visit, play, and take pictures:

- Pam Stefanich, family child care provider, Learning to Grow Daycare

- Lynette Lohan, family child care provider, Lohan Family Child Care

- Beach Husk, director, Native American Child Care Center (NAEYC accredited)

- Donella Busker, owner, The Peaceful Place Child Care Center

- Erika McWell, director, Stella Sanford Child Development Center (NAEYC accredited)

Thanks to Debby Bullis and Pam Stefanich for sharing project ideas. Your creativity is greatly appreciated.

Oh, and thanks to everyone at Redleaf Press for their hard work on this book. Your dedication to supporting the profession of early care and education is unequaled. Extra special thanks to Cathy Broberg for her editing expertise. Her fresh eyes were vital in transforming the original manuscript into a real book.

Introduction

They Play with the Box It Came In

Birthdays, Christmas, Chanukah, I-Bought-You-This-So-You-Wouldn't-Whine-and-Make-a-Scene-Day: you name the gift-giving occasion and odds are children will have as much fun with the box a gift came in as with their shiny new store-bought toy. That empty cardboard box holds more than a new toy; it holds a world of possibility. If you've spent any time with a child, you've seen it happen: empty boxes become race cars, spaceships, bathtubs, baby beds, boats, suitcases, robot suits, castles, dinosaur cages, and eagle nests. Anything children can imagine—or happen to need to further their play—is right there in that empty box. The toy that came in that box—even if it is marketed as an educational toy—probably offers far less flexibility, creative stimulation, excitement, and fun than the box does.

The following projects were designed to emulate the creative possibilities of an empty box. All the projects that made it into the book passed the Empty Box Test for children ages five and under:

- The materials are simple, inexpensive, and readily available.

- Children find them engaging, flexible, exciting, and stimulating.

- Children can engage in play without too much adult instruction and intervention.

- Children choose to come back to the activities again and again to play, explore, and discover.

These projects were developed through my experience as a child care provider. All of the projects are appropriate for use in such a setting but they can also be used by any caregiver of young children in any setting.

Learning through Play

The activities and projects in this book all have one thing in common: they promote learning through play. In a world that is becoming increasingly focused on standardized tests, measurements, and pushing children to their limits, this book offers a simple alternative for everyday learning.

The best thing we can do to promote learning with young children is provide them with a physical and emotional environment that is warm, engaging, inviting, fun, healthy, and safe. When we do this, we hear the joyful sounds of learning. Children play, explore, and discover. They ask questions and seek out their own answers.

Be Ready to Explain Yourself

No matter who you are, you're going to have some explaining to do when you play with these projects. If you have been working with children in a child care setting for more than a week, you have at least some understanding of the constant need for documenting learning and defending curriculum with parents, administrators, regulators, and funders. If you've been in the field for a long time, you're probably accustomed to explaining yourself to the people who pass through your classroom.

Even if you're using these projects with your own children in the privacy of your own home, you are probably going to have to explain yourself to someone at some time. Grandma is going to have questions when she sees three-year-old Sally making the lid repeatedly explode off a film canister using a bit of water and an antacid tablet.

It's important that you can explain to anyone who asks what the children are learning as they play. I'll describe the learning taking place in each activity later in the book. In the meantime, here is what you need to do:

- Feel comfortable and confident explaining yourself to anyone who asks questions. Whether you are talking to Grandma, a parent, your program's director, or a senator, you should feel at ease answering questions about what is going on in your learning environment. Developing this sense of comfort and confidence takes time and practice. Start by being on the lookout for the learning going on around you all the time. When you get used to identifying it for yourself, you will be more comfortable pointing it out for others.

- Observe, observe, observe. Knowing how individual children play and learn will not only help you explain what they are learning when the need arises, but will also help you better meet the needs of the individual learners in your care. You will notice ways to challenge them and build on their prior knowledge.

- Never miss an opportunity to increase your own knowledge about how children learn. The more you know, the more comfortable you will be discussing early learning and the better you will be at helping it happen.

- Document learning through portfolios of work, photography, video, or by other unobtrusive means. Taking the time to develop an appropriate and systematic method will help you explain your practices. You have to know what you are doing, know what the kids are learning, and know how to explain yourself to those who question your process and practices.

Steps to Nurturing Play, Exploration, and Learning

Loving and caring teachers create safe havens for their children. In such sacred communities, children are welcomed, appreciated, and respected.

—Mimi Brodsky Chenfeld,
Creative Experiences for Young Children

Creating an emotional environment conducive to play and filling it with materials that pass the Empty Box Test sets the stage for everyday early learning. When children feel emotionally and physically safe and are surrounded by interesting materials, learning simply happens. Children in this type of learning environment thrive cognitively, physically, socially, and emotionally. Such an environment for young children takes full advantage of what we know about brain development in the first five years of life: it lays a solid foundation of learning success in preparation for school and life.

Here are some of the keys to creating a strong and sturdy early learning environment:

1. Provide time

2. Offer freedom and control

3. Avoid pressure

4. Feed interests and enthusiasm

5. Make learning meaningful

6. Assure emotional safety

7. Give encouragement and support

These steps address the emotional environment you create for children rather than the physical environment. Creating an emotional environment that promotes early learning means building an atmosphere of trust. This will serve as a foundation for helping children make their play experiences quality learning experiences.

The emotional environment is at least as important as the physical environment. Early learning can, and does, happen in all kinds of locations—child care centers, city parks, Grandma's kitchen table—if the following measures are taken to create the right emotional environment.

Provide Time

Children who spend their lives rushing from home to babysitter to child care center to swimming lessons to dance lessons experience the antithesis of what children experience in play. During play children are in control of what is going on, and the pace is of their own making.

—Lilian Katz and Diane McClellan,
Fostering Children's Social Competence

In today's world, younger and younger children are being rushed from one preplanned, adult-driven, overly regimented activity to the next. Their hyperscheduled days allow less and less time for leisurely play, exploration, and discovery. Yet children need—and do their best learning in—large blocks of unscheduled time when they are able to choose their own activities and proceed at a leisurely pace. Such time allows freedom to fully explore materials, test ideas, repeat activities and actions, contemplate, imagine, reflect, and grow. Large chunks of time spent with activities or materials children have selected for themselves also helps them learn to focus and concentrate, and serves to increase their attention span.

Offer Freedom and Control

In his play world, the young child is the decision-maker and the play-master. There are no superimposed directions to follow, no rigid rules to which to adhere.

—Frank and Theresa Caplan, *The Power of Play*

Freedom and control over actions and activities must be a part of real play. This doesn't mean abdicating your responsibilities as a caregiver and letting the children do whatever they want, unsupervised. Rules and limits need to be set to assure the children's safety and further their social development. But it's important to balance our concern for safety and desire not to have our home or center destroyed with the children's need for an optimal learning environment. If children are given too much freedom and control, things can quickly deteriorate into a state of chaos; if they are not given enough freedom and control, their learning can be severely stifled.

Learning to manage freedom and be in control are two of the most important things a young child can learn. Freedom to make choices concerning play is practice for making good choices in life. Having control over the play process teaches a child to be a leader and decision maker. It also provides a chance to practice the most important control of all: *self*-control. These skills are much more important than differentiating between a green ball and a blue ball. They also take much more practice and time to master. Having freedom and control not only allows children to learn more during play, it helps children learn self-regulation, build confidence, make good decisions, think independently, and develop leadership skills.

Avoid Pressure

While we can sometimes encourage children to become interested in new things, we must be careful not to usurp children's freedom to choose their own activities and the peers with whom they will do those activities.

—Bev Bos, *Together We're Better*

As a parent, I have repeatedly caught myself guiding my children toward activities and interests *I* would like them to pursue and love. It takes great effort to step back and let them make their own choices and it is exceedingly easy to find yourself applying undue pressure. Children should be allowed to choose their activities, interests, friends, pastimes, and direction as much as possible, and they should be able to do it without pressure from the adults in their lives. We should also avoid pressuring them about their performance. Remember this: they are kids and their learning should be fun, relaxed, and pressure free.

Feed Interests and Enthusiasm

Children are easily engaged in activities about which they are interested and enthusiastic. This engagement expands their understanding and knowledge, increases their attention span, deepens their ability to focus, and drives learning. My little buddy Jack loves bugs. I've seen him spend hours and hours exploring my yard on warm spring mornings discovering, catching, examining, explaining, running from, and running to different insects. He is in what is referred to as "the zone" or "a state of flow" when he plays with bugs; he's fully immersed in what he is doing.

When children show special interest in a topic, activity, book, color, toy, food, character, animal, toothpaste, rock, or anything else that catches their eye, we need to find a way to feed that interest. Think about it for a minute and you'll probably be able to identify a bug kid, car kid, cat kid, dinosaur kid, doll kid, marker kid, magnet kid, and balloon kid who has passed through your life. Sometimes their interest and enthusiasm about something lasts a few minutes and other times it lasts a lifetime.

Make Learning Meaningful

None of us like investing our limited time and energy in activities that are not meaningful. Forcing children to take part in an activity they find meaningless is a sure way to add stress to your day. If, however, you can make that activity meaningful to the children in some way, you will find that they readily participate. If you cannot think of a way to give the activity meaning to the children, and they find no meaning in it themselves, it might be time to shelve that activity. Too many caregivers force children to take part in trite, hollow, stale activities that are devoid of meaning. You can see the distaste for such activities in the glazed eyes of the children. When we make learning meaningful, their eyes blaze with joy and excitement, they glow with energy and enthusiasm. Like adults, children find meaning in the things they connect to on an emotional or intellectual level. When this connection is present, the activity becomes meaningful and the children will buy into it.

Assure Emotional Safety

A strong relationship between child and caregiver is one of the keys to a successful early learning experience. Such a relationship makes building an environment where the child feels emotionally safe much simpler. Children whose emotional needs are met are more at ease and better able to focus on opportunities for play, exploration, and discovery. A child who is constantly on guard emotionally, on the other hand, is unable to focus on anything other than the emotional dynamic of the room. Time invested in building a strong emotional tie with each child and assuring they all feel safe enough to be themselves is hard work, but it is well worth the time and effort.

Give Encouragement and Support

Your encouraging words are like a magic tonic to a young child—they promote her confidence during exploratory play; they galvanize her motivation to persist at difficult learning tasks.

—Alice Sterling Honig, *Secure Relationships*

Encouragement and support also help build the emotionally safe environments that children need. When we encourage and support children in their play, we are telling them they are heading in the right direction, are people of value, are an important part of the group, and are doing a bang-up job at being children. We can give this support with our words, our eyes, our smiles, and our actions. It doesn't matter much how we encourage them as long as we do encourage them.

Become a Professional Play Technician

Another way you can promote early learning is by thinking of yourself as a professional play technician. Don't let the words *professional* and *technician* scare you. All I am asking is that you approach play with proficiency and competence. You should develop skills, deepen your understanding, and expand your knowledge relating to how children play. Become a person skilled at playing. You don't need to be an expert; heck, if you're reading this book and can remember being a child, you probably already know more than you think. Work on honing the play skills you might have forgotten you had and maybe add some depth to that current knowledge so you can make the most of the following activities.

It's *All* Curriculum

I've talked about the importance of creating the right emotional environment for early learning and stocking that environment with materials that pass the Empty Box Test in preparation for optimal early learning experiences. Here's an example of how it works in the family child care program my wife and I operate.

One day while the kids finished lunch, I prepared for water play, something that always passes the Empty Box Test. In fact, we like water play so much that we added a custom built-in water-play table to our family child care playroom that is the perfect height for the children and has its own drain and hot and cold running water. On this day I decided to add a big mound of shredded paper to the water for no other reason than that I needed to empty my office shredder. By this time the kids were done with lunch and ready to play. Busy hands pressed the pile of paper into the warm water and formed it into snowballs, donuts, and other shapes. Someone sculpted a person out of mushy paper.

As they played, the paper began to dissolve into a pulpy gray mess. Questions flew: Why did you put this paper in the water? Why is the paper falling apart? How do they make paper anyway? How will we get the paper out of the sink? Will it clog the drain like last time? What happens if we squeeze the paper gunk really hard? On and on they went. Sometimes I could squeeze an answer in between questions, sometimes they found their own answers, sometimes the questions just drifted off because there was a fresh one on someone's lips.

Then five-year-old Jack asked, "Jeff, can *you* make paper?" I answered that I could indeed make paper and that I could teach him to do it too if he liked. This idea was met with universal approval and a ringing chorus of "Me too?"

So, as the younger children headed off to take their naps, the older children and I began making paper with the pulpy goop from the water table (see pages 24–25 to learn to make your own paper). This led to more questions about the paper-making process, discussions about engineering and science, chatter about writing and drawing on the paper we were making, speculation about what life would be like without paper, lists of different kinds of paper, ideas to make our fresh paper dry faster, a scheme to start a paper-making business, suggestions to make our paper prettier and stronger, and much more. After I showed them the process, they took over and spent the afternoon making paper. The next day, those children helped some of the younger kids make paper. They also made use of the paper they had made the day before in writing, drawing, and craft projects. The paper-making activities lasted for days and made it into this book because, like water play, it passed the Empty Box Test.

It is hardly surprising that this very simple water-play activity evolved into a multiday project that allowed the children to expand their skills and knowledge. *Everything* that takes place in a quality early learning environment is part of the curriculum, whether it is planned or not. I had no preconceived intention or inclination to make paper that day, but Jack's question guided us in that direction. The children showed an interest that we were able to build off, which led us to new knowledge and skills. That's how early learning should happen.

Children are learning all the time and they are usually learning more than one thing at once. In the example above, the children worked on their language skills, physical skills, social skills, thinking skills, problem-solving skills, and creativity as we played in the water and made paper. They were learning all those things all at once as part of the process. It was messy, often loud, not as organized as most adults would like, and there was constant motion. I have to admit that at times it may have seemed chaotic to an onlooker, but that's how early learning looks at times. We made a mess, there was lots of motion, we were loud at times, things might have looked disorganized, but learning was right underneath that chaotic veneer.

Using the Activities

Storage and Organization

I once heard about a caregiver who had too much storage space for all her play equipment and materials, but I've been unable to verify the story and figure it is one of those Internet myths. Parents and providers are always at the mercy of the available storage space when considering new materials. Ask a child care provider what they would like most in their program space and "more storage" will be in the top five every time. Ask a parent looking for a new home

what they want that home to have and "more storage space" will be in the top five again. Even if you have ample space, finding what you want when you want it is another constant battle. With these issues in mind, I have tried to make the items that follow easy to store and organize.

I recommend storing most projects in plastic freezer bags and clear plastic totes. If you use one-gallon freezer bags and then store those bags in the clear plastic tote, you should be able to find things quickly when you want them.

Cost

You can spend lots of money on over-priced products from catalogs and toy stores if you like, but it's not really necessary. My goal here was to keep material costs under $10 per project. Most items are much less than that, while a few cost more.

Where to Shop

You can purchase the materials needed for most of these projects where you usually shop. I purchased materials at our local "super-center," grocery store, dollar store, and on the Internet. There were also a few things I needed to run to the hardware store for and some things were scavenged from our recycling bin.

Activity Organization

Children are comfortable learning many things at once amid what most grownups consider chaos, but our adult minds usually prefer to process information in a more orderly and structured manner. For that reason, the activities that follow have been divided into these categories: Language and Literacy, Math and Logical Thinking, Science and Problem Solving, Creative Expression and Thinking, Social Skills and Relationships, and Physical Skills. Sometimes an activity's placement is arbitrary; you will find that most activities would fit comfortably in more than one chapter.

Activity Components

Ages

Each activity lists a general age range the project is intended for, but remember, all kids are unique and you need to use your own judgment about when a child is developmentally ready for an activity. Children will approach activities and materials differently based on their age, development level, and personal preferences. In some cases, younger children may not be able to work with a project the same way an older child will but they can benefit from it nonetheless. Also remember that kids can change fast. A child may show no interest in a particular activity one day but find it deeply meaningful a day or week later.

Ease of Construction

Each activity has a rating of 1 to 3. Here is what those ratings mean:

= Super simple. Buy the materials, put them in front of the kids, and get out of the way.

= Easy, but not effortless. Although some construction or modification to materials is required, power tools are not.

= Worth the work. These projects either have a few more construction steps or require power tools. They aren't really complicated; they just may be outside some people's comfort zone. If you don't want to take on one of these projects yourself, you likely know people who would. It should not be too hard to convince them to help: just show them the project description, say "the kids would really appreciate it" in your sweetest voice, and offer them some pizza, an adult beverage, or other inducement. Heck, these may end up being the *easiest* projects for you to complete!

Description

Here you'll find a few paragraphs explaining what the project is all about as well as details and stories about how children engage with the materials.

Learning

Because being able to explain your teaching rational is so important, this section looks at what children learn when they use the activities and projects. You can always look here if someone asks a question like "Why is Aaliyah playing with *that*?" This is probably the most important heading for those of you who are fighting daily battles to preserve play in the lives of young children. You may, however, find that children are learning more than what is listed here.

Materials

This is your shopping list for each project, a nice short list of things you need.

Instructions

This is a numbered list of steps you will take to complete the project.

Safety Notes

Some activities require a bit more supervision or care. Safety notes are included when a safety reminder is needed.

Variations

Under this heading you will find—surprise!—variations for using the materials. These are often things I didn't initially think of but saw the children do when they got their hands on the stuff. I also suggest other items you can add to the mix to extend children's play and different ideas for getting the most bang for your buck.

Other Tips

Here are some final tips for getting the most out of the projects:

- When possible, let older children help shop for or gather the materials for the projects. This engages them in the activity from the very beginning and creates additional learning opportunities. I know field trips can be tough, but the potential for learning (especially language and social skills) makes it worth the effort.

- Older children can take the lead in preparing the materials for play. My child care buddy Pam from South Dakota says the schoolagers in her program built many of the projects from my book *Do-It-Yourself Early Learning*. In an e-mail, she shared the following: "I asked them to review the book, choosing items they would like to build. After reading and viewing the various options, they began writing up materials lists. As a team, we then headed to the nearest hardware store where we found and purchased our supplies. With supervision, they went about building their favorite projects in the book. I still remember the pride on their faces when their projects were completed." Pam said all the kids in her program enjoyed the projects the older children had built.

- Don't introduce too many new activities at once; it can overwhelm the children and make it difficult for them to focus. The goal is to give them the chance to fully explore and get to know the materials. It is hard to get any kind of deep engagement when kids are trying to focus on too much input.

- Let the children discover the materials when possible. We introduce most new dramatic play props and manipulatives to the children in our program by placing them on a shelf the night before and waiting to see what happens when they are discovered. Allowing children to discover new materials is exciting for them, it gives them control and ownership, and most of all it is great fun to sit back and see how they act and react.

- Don't worry if kids don't use something "right." Unless they are doing something potentially dangerous to themselves or someone else, let it go. Exploration and discovery are what we are after; you never know what someone's personal history, knowledge, and unique perspective will bring to the materials.

- Use your own ideas too. Don't hesitate to build off the following projects using your own ideas and knowledge. See where your ideas take you. The key to these projects is their flexibility; don't think for a second that you have to rigorously adhere to my suggestions and ideas. Use what follows as a starting point for your own adventure in early learning.

MEET ZOË

Hi, I'm Zoë. Jeff's my dad and I've helped him think up lots of the projects in this book. I've also helped test them out with kids and have even helped demonstrate them to child care providers at conferences. I'll be popping in every once in a while throughout the book to add my opinion or tell a story. My dad is almost done rambling on about early learning—that means the projects are coming up really soon. Stay tuned.

A Note on Safety

Child safety is a concern in all early learning environments. My goal has been to develop activities for this book that are safe for use by average children under average supervision in average play environments. Each activity considered for this book was taken for a test drive in our family child care program. Most made the cut as originally conceived, but some failed to stand up under the rigorous use of real live children (real live children with extremely close and alert supervision, of course). While they all passed the Empty Box Test with flying colors, some items were not as durable as I would have liked and a few had other flaws that made them unsafe. The ideas that didn't work on their initial test drive were sent back to the shop for more work. We managed to hammer the kinks out of most of them pretty quickly, but there were some we just could not save. The items that made the cut for inclusion in this book are used regularly in our program and many were test-driven in other settings as well. Any concerns arising from those subsequent tests were addressed so that we could make safe recommendations. Notes on any activity-specific safety concerns are included with the individual projects.

The most important part of child safety when using these materials is adult supervision. These activities are meant to be well supervised by an adult. If you give children the materials and fail to appropriately supervise their play, you are putting them at risk of injury.

Here are some general safety notes:

- Make the health and safety of the children your priority at all times. Keep their ongoing physical well-being in the forefront of your thoughts.

- The children in your care are only as safe as you make them. Appropriate adult supervision and observation is the key to child safety in most circumstances; this holds true for these projects as well. Keep your eyes and ears open and your mind focused on the activity at hand.

- Know the children and make adjustments to the projects as needed. One benefit that comes with building strong emotional relationships with the children you care for is that you learn to understand how they play. Get to know which

children are risk takers, which ones are more likely to put things in their mouths, which ones let their curiosity put them in potentially dangerous situations, and which are most likely to need additional supervision.

Conclusion

I don't have the solution to the various problems and challenges facing our nation's educational system or know how to slow down the harried pace many children face so early in life. However, I do know what we're going to do in my little corner of the world: spend large hunks of time climbing apple trees, getting muddy, hunting for bugs, running, falling, skinning our knees, and just being kids. We are going to observe birds and bugs and bunnies in all their birdie-ness, buggy-ness, and bunny-ness, and learn a ton while doing so. We are also going to learn social skills, science, language, problem solving, math, logical thinking, and healthy living while we're at it (without even knowing we are learning!). We are going to learn the way early learning is supposed to happen: by playing.

I hope you enjoy the activities—thanks for reading. Now, play, explore, and discover.

Promoting
Language and Literacy

Are you going to the pet store after you drop the kids off? My mom doesn't take me to the pet store enough. They have turtles at the pet store. Jeff, you should buy another car seat and take me to the pet store.

—Ty, age 2½, as I headed out the door to take some older children to school

The most powerful tools adults can give children are words. The activities in this chapter —and the whole of this book—will help children build their vocabularies and improve their use of language. Among other things, strong language skills empower children to ask questions, solve problems, interact with others, name and understand their feelings and emotions, and share ideas. Language is the foundation for all other learning. Children learn this quickly. Toddlers who stand next to an adult, lift their hands in the air, and utter the word "up" are instantly lifted into the air and hugged. The word "more" from the same toddler brings additional bits of banana. Simply saying "mama" or "dada" for the first time is enough to stop parents in their tracks. Words equal power.

This chapter includes a wide variety of book-building projects because it is important to get books in the hands of children every day. Doing so helps them develop a habit of handling, using, and enjoying books early on. Some of the projects promote prereading skills while others help children inch ever closer to reading on their own.

Create the books in these activities and then make them available to the kids. Certainly have a story time or two during the day, but in addition put these books out where the kids can get to them, play with them, feel them, and begin reading them on their own.

Learning the Feel of Language

Ages: 3+

Ease of Construction

Description While most children are primarily visual or auditory learners, some are tactile or kinetic learners. They learn best by touching, feeling, and manipulating objects. By building language with cotton swabs or toothpicks instead of paper and pencils, kids begin to develop a physical and mental feel for words.

Learning This activity helps children, especially tactile learners, internalize the shapes of letters and words and learn to distinguish between positive and negative space as well as develop small-muscle skills, hand-eye coordination, and logical thinking. It also helps children improve comprehension.

Materials

☐ Index cards

☐ Marker

☐ Bobby pins, cotton swabs, or toothpicks

Instructions

1. On each index card write a letter or word the children use often.

2. When you have a nice selection, ask the children to re-create the letters or words using toothpicks, bobby pins, or cotton swabs. Show them the card with the letter A and make a toothpick A as an example. They should catch on quickly and go right to work. Be there to help if needed, but try to stay out of the way and let them work. You will need to use a bit of imagination for letters with curves. Think about the numbers on a digital clock and simply square up the rounded sections of the letters.

SAFETY NOTE *Although some would view these manipulatives as a potential hazard, they are great learning tools when used with supervision. Remember, almost anything can be dangerous to young children. Supervision is the key.*

Variations

■ Challenge the kids to make huge letters, medium-size letters, or small letters. You might need to move to the floor for this. It takes some space to write your name in six-foot-long cotton swab letters.

■ Let them be creative and use the materials to create pictures of people, pets, or places they know.

■ Turn the tables and let the kids suggest words for you to re-create.

■ How about creating roads and parking places for toy cars out of bobby pins? This is still part of learning language because it helps kids distinguish positive space (bobby pins) from negative space (table top), which is what they are doing when they read print on a page.

■ Challenge older children to write a whole story using toothpicks.

■ When you're outside, use rocks, blades of grass, or small sticks.

freezer Bag Books

Ages: 3+

Ease of Construction

Description Young children can be incredibly tough on traditional books. Their eagerness to explore the pictures and words often results in ripped pages. Here is a project that uses everyday materials to make strong, durable, and inexpensive books that young children can use until they can be trusted with "real" books. As a bonus, older children can make their own books and tell their own stories using this easy method.

Learning Using these durable books helps young children learn to properly care for and handle books. They will also develop important prereading skills that set the stage for a lifelong love of books. Older children will find they can be writers as well as readers. They will learn how to make their own books. This is very empowering and serves to deepen their knowledge, love, and understanding of written language.

Materials

- ☐ Cardstock
- ☐ Scissors
- ☐ Six to eight heavy-duty ziplock freezer bags, 1-quart size
- ☐ Markers, construction paper, glue, and other craft supplies
- ☐ Stapler
- ☐ Duct tape

Instructions

1. Cut the cardstock so it will easily slip inside the freezer bags. These will become the pages of your book. You will need two pieces of cardstock for each freezer bag.

2. Use your craft supplies to add words and images to one side of each piece of card stock. The zipper side of the bag will be the spine of the book, so make sure you orient the pages properly.

3. Place two pages into each freezer bag.

4. Zip the bags shut and staple them together along the zipper to form a book.

5. Add a strip of duct tape around the stapled edge to reinforce the spine and protect little fingers from the staples.

6. Let the children enjoy reading the books.

SAFETY NOTE *Although these books are quite tough, they still need to be used with supervision, especially for infants and toddlers with new teeth who may chew the plastic bags.*

Variations

- Invite older children to compose and construct their own books.
- Make books the children can take home with them.
- See pages 14, 19, and 22 for other variations of this type of book.

Environmental Print Books

Ages: 3+

Ease of Construction

Description Environmental print is the writing we see all around us, on signs, cereal and juice boxes, laundry detergent jugs, and so on. Often kids who can't read yet already know what it represents. Most two-year-olds know what those golden arches on the red background mean as soon as they spy the sign with their little eyes. This project uses environmental print as an aid to encourage reading in young children.

Learning Environmental print books promote prereading skills: letter and word recognition, visual decoding, and basic book etiquette. Learning to read is a process that includes learning how to hold books, turn the pages, and read from left to right and top to bottom. These books also build confidence and a history of reading success. They lay the groundwork for reading more advanced books.

Materials

- ☐ Environmental print from boxes, bags, and other common packaging
- ☐ Scissors
- ☐ Six to eight heavy-duty ziplock freezer bags, 1-quart size
- ☐ Stapler
- ☐ Duct tape

Instructions

1. Cut your environmental print so it fits into the freezer bags.
2. Place two pieces of environmental print into each freezer bag. The zipper side of the bag will be the spine of the book, so make sure you orient the materials properly.
3. Zip the bags shut and staple them together along the zipper to form a book.
4. Add a strip of duct tape around the stapled edge to reinforce the spine and protect little fingers from the staples.
5. Place the books on the children's bookshelf for them to read.

Variations

- Add food boxes with environmental print to dramatic play areas.
- Let older kids cut out the letters or words they know or recognize from magazines, boxes, or paper bags.
- Point out environmental print to children as you go about your day and ask if they can read it to you.
- Use pages from magazines and catalogs to create books on themes that interest the children—food, tools, cars, motorcycles, whatever.
- Create environmental print books on topics like nutrition, fitness, families, and animals.

My full name is Zoë Lou Johnson. I'm fourteen years old, well at least I am when I'm writing this; I'll be older by the time you read it. I live in Sioux City, Iowa—I have for my entire life. I'm homeschooled. I've been in tae kwon do since I was seven.

I've grown up in the child care programs my mom and dad have run and now that I am older I help them out sometimes. It's cool to see the little kids learn new stuff while they are playing. I also like going to conferences and trainings with my dad and teaching adults how to play. They get the same looks on their faces as the kids do when they learn something new.

Well, that's all the useless and uninteresting things about me, so I'll fill you in on the more exciting stuff. I speak Sindarn and for those of you who don't know what that is (which is most likely everybody), it's a form of Elvish. You see, I like The Lord of the Rings, *but who could blame me? They're good books and movies. I also like* Harry Potter, Star Wars, *and vampires. I crochet, knit (I taught myself), latch hook, embroider, sew, and I can do some card tricks. I guess you could call me nerdy, but the fact that I listen to awesome music kind of balances out my nerdiness.*

Sheet Protector Books

Ages: 2+

Ease of Construction

Description Clear plastic sheet protectors are another useful material in creating durable and inexpensive children's books. My wife, Tasha, and I have used them for years in our family child care program as well as in center-based and school-age programs. When she was younger, our daughter Zoë published a number of her own books using the directions that follow.

Learning These books will help build prereading and reading skills. They will also help children develop small-muscle skills, hand-eye coordination, creativity, and a love of books. Like the other bookmaking projects in this chapter, this project will empower children as readers and writers.

Materials

- ☐ Paper, 8½ by 11 inches
- ☐ Markers, pens, crayons, paint, and other craft supplies
- ☐ Plastic sheet protectors
- ☐ Tape
- ☐ Stapler
- ☐ Duct tape

Instructions

1. Use the paper and craft materials to create two book pages for every sheet protector you plan to use. Make sure to create a book cover as well.

2. Insert two book pages into each sheet protector.

3. Tape the open side of each sheet protector shut so the pages stay in place.

4. Staple the sheet protectors together. Make sure your pages are in the proper order.

5. Add a strip of duct tape around the stapled edge to reinforce the spine and protect little fingers from the staples.

6. Let the children read the books.

Variations

- ■ Instead of stapling the pages together, place them into a three-ring binder or use three keychain rings to bind the pages together.

- ■ This is a great way to make children's art into picture books; just slip their creations into sheet protectors, tape the top, bind it, and stick it on the bookshelf. It's important to display children's artwork and this is a simple and effective way to make sure they can see it and share it whenever they like.

- ■ Use your computer and printer to create pages with a more finished look.

craft-Stick Books

Ages: 3 +

Ease of Construction

Description Kids love to make their own books and this is a simple and straightforward way for them to do so. Once they learn the basic process, they'll be hooked on publishing their own books. These books are not as durable as freezer bag and sheet protector books, so they are better for older children who have some experience caring for books properly.

Learning Using these books will empower older children and encourage them to use words and tell their own stories. They build language, small-muscle, and comprehension skills, and practice creative expression.

Materials

- ☐ Paper, 8½ by 11 inches
- ☐ Hole punch
- ☐ Rubber bands
- ☐ Craft sticks
- ☐ Pens, markers, and other craft materials

Instructions

1. For each book, fold five pieces of paper in half to make rectangles 8½ inches by 5½ inches.

2. Use the hole punch to make two holes about 4 inches apart along the folded side of the paper.

3. Thread a rubber band through the holes from the top.

4. On the back of the book, loop the rubber band over the ends of a craft stick to secure it in place.

5. Now let the children use the craft supplies and their imaginations to fill the pages of their books.

Variations

- Create a bunch of blank books to have around for younger children to write in.

- Allow children to cut pictures out of magazines and catalogs and then glue them into the craft-stick books.

- Invite older children to make these books and use them as journals or diaries. Encourage them to write in them every day. You may want to make books with more pages for this activity.

Colorful Felt Books

Ages: Infancy to 3

Ease of Construction

Description These bright and durable books are simple rectangles of colored felt stitched together. Young children will sit and fiddle with them, modeling older readers. Slightly older children will read the books to you from cover to cover, confidently naming the color of each page. You can read these books to children by naming and talking about each color.

Learning This type of book offers a simple way to introduce very young children to the concept of "book," even before they begin talking. Among other things, it gives them a chance to learn about turning pages, reading from left to right, treating books nicely, and putting them away when they are done. Children will be developing valuable prereading skills such as learning to enjoy books and becoming aware of sounds using books that don't even have words. They will also develop vocabulary from listening to others "read" the wordless books.

Materials

☐ Felt in various colors

☐ Scissors

☐ Needle and thread

Instructions

1. Cut the felt into 6-inch squares. We usually use six to eight squares of felt for each book.

2. Arrange them in a neat stack.

3. Use the needle and thread to securely stitch the pieces of felt together along one side.

4. Give these soft books to the infants and toddlers for them to explore.

Variations

■ Let older children make these books for younger kids to use.

■ Try embroidering letters, numbers, or words onto the felt pages. Or write on the pages with markers.

■ Use a sewing machine if you have one.

Environmental Object Books

Ages: 3+

Ease of Construction

Description Here's another project that helps kids learn to love books and words, this time using everyday objects like plastic blocks, toy cars, markers, playdough, craft sticks, and other materials kids know. The books are easy for young children to "read" because the items contained in the pages are from their world.

Learning These books help kids develop prereading skills and build vocabularies. They empower children to use language confidently. The items used in these books create a starting point for conversations and questions that lead to even more vocabulary building and understanding of the world. Because they will be able to feel the items through the plastic pages, this is a very tactile book and good for children who learn through the sense of touch. One version of this book we made at our house had a large lump of playdough in it that the children could manipulate as we read.

Materials

- ☐ Small objects the children can identify (toy cars, crayons, rubber bands, keys, baby spoons, empty glue bottles)
- ☐ Six to eight heavy-duty ziplock freezer bags, 1-quart size
- ☐ Stapler
- ☐ Duct tape
- ☐ Scissors

Instructions

1. Place one environmental object in each freezer bag.

2. Zip the bags shut and staple them together along the zipper to form a book.

3. Add a strip of duct tape around the stapled edge to reinforce the spine and protect little fingers from the staples.

4. Let the children explore the books.

Variations

- ■ Make theme books: blocks, kitchen items, cars, action figures.
- ■ Let each child select items for a special book.
- ■ Look at these books with infants and toddlers. Be sure to supervise closely so they don't put the plastic bags in their mouths.

fabric Sensory Books

Ages: Infancy to 3

Ease of Construction

Description Younger kids love books that stimulate many of their senses at once. These books are exciting for kids to touch, they make noise, and they're fun to look at. The books are also relatively easy to make and will stand up to lots of hands-on use.

Learning Paging through these fun books helps children learn book basics as well as sensory perception.

Materials

☐ Fabric, different types and textures

☐ Pinking shears

☐ Sewing machine or needle and thread

☐ Aluminum foil

☐ Plastic shopping bags

☐ Newspaper

Instructions

1. Use pinking shears to cut the fabric into 8- to 10-inch squares. You will need two squares of fabric for each page of your book.

2. Pair the squares together, with the right side of the fabric facing out.

3. Stitch along three sides of each pair of squares to form pages.

4. Through the open side of each page, stuff newspaper, aluminum foil, or plastic bags.

5. Stitch the open side of each page shut.

6. Stack the pages and stitch them together on the left edge to create the book.

7. Place the books where babies or children can reach them.

Variations

■ How about adding jingle bells to a page?

■ Try adding wooden blocks, milk jug lids, plastic jar lids, bouncy balls, and other items so children can feel the shapes and try to guess what is inside the pages.

■ If you're using a sewing machine and making small stitches, use rice or dried beans inside a page.

Gift-Card Books

Ages: Infancy +

Ease of Construction

Description This is a simple way to recycle old plastic gift cards, expired library, gym, and other ID cards, and hotel key cards into environmental print books. They have been very popular with the children in our program and in other child care settings we have visited.

Learning These small books help kids learn about letter recognition, decoding language, and other prereading skills.

Materials

☐ Old plastic gift cards, ID cards, and hotel key cards

☐ Hole punch

☐ Metal key ring (available at craft stores)

Instructions

1. Using the hole punch, make a hole in one corner of each card about ½ inch from the edge.

2. Attach the cards together with the key ring.

Variations

■ Leave these books in your dramatic play area. Older children will use them as credit cards in their dramatic play, and they will inspire all kinds of conversations and language development.

■ If you build up a large enough collection of these cards, use them for a variety of different matching and memory games. Ask parents and others to donate their cards to the cause.

counting Books

Ages: 3+

Ease of Construction

Description This project will create four counting books using a deck of cards and the bookmaking techniques used earlier in this chapter.

Learning This book will help children develop prereading skills and become aware of numbers, shapes, and colors.

Materials

☐ Deck of playing cards

☐ Clear ziplock craft bags, 3 by 5 inches (available in big-box stores and craft stores)

☐ Stapler

☐ Duct tape

☐ Scissors

Instructions

1. Toss aside the face cards—you won't need them for this project. We usually add them to the box of scrap paper we keep for cutting and gluing.

2. Place one card into each bag and zip shut.

3. Arrange the bags by suit and then put each suit in numerical order.

4. Staple the zipper edge of each stack.

5. Add a strip of duct tape around the stapled edge to reinforce the spine and protect little fingers from the staples. You have just created four counting books.

Variations

■ Instead of cards, use colored marbles, pebbles, or pennies in your counting books. (To prevent choking, make sure the small objects stay in the bags.)

■ Take pictures of children holding up fingers and toes and use them to make a counting book. Can the children identify who all the pinkies and piggies belong to?

■ Use clear contact paper and craft sticks to make a counting book. Just sandwich different numbers of sticks between sheets of contact paper to make individual pages and use staples and duct tape to bind the pages together.

■ Instead of bags, use a hole punch and a key ring to make these books for older children. Follow the directions for the previous activity, Gift-Card Books.

Early Literacy from the Recycling Bin

Ages: Infancy +

Ease of Construction

Description We keep a selection of old catalogs, magazines, and newspapers on hand—and within reach—so that the little people we don't quite trust with our fancy store-bought books always have something they can read. Infants and toddlers like to shake them and rip the pages. Preschoolers and older children look at the pictures and feed their imaginations.

Learning Paging through catalogs, magazines, and newspapers helps infants, toddlers, and pre-schoolers develop prereading and prewriting skills as well as fine-motor skills. These materials help older children build stronger vocabularies and hone reading and writing skills. They are also a great prop for inspiring creative play.

Materials

☐ Old catalogs, magazines, and newspapers

Instructions

1. Keep a stack of these materials in your bookshelf, craft area, dramatic play area, or another location where children have ready access to them.

2. Let the children use them in their play and be available to answer questions like "Will you buy me this?" "What's that?" and "Can we go here?"

Variations

■ Let the kids cut out pictures and glue them to paper. (Cutting and gluing are great prewriting skills because they develop hand muscles.)

■ Give older children highlighters and ask them to highlight letters or words they know.

■ Have older children cut out words from headlines and headings and use them to "write" new sentences.

■ Let children trace letters and pictures. This activity is especially fun if you have a light table available.

Papermaking

Ages: 3+

Ease of Construction

Description Although there are lots of steps to this project, and making good paper takes practice, it's not hard and the kids will love it. In this activity, kids, like my buddy Jack from the introduction, transform goopy, soggy old shredded paper into brand new paper sheets. The process is as much fun as the final product.

Learning Children will use their creativity, small and large muscles, and imaginations. They will have a chance to practice both following directions and being patient—papermaking is not a quick process. They can also practice their writing skills when the paper is finally done.

Materials

- Paper (newspaper, old coloring book pages, wrapping paper, construction paper, paper bags, or whatever you have lying around)
- Water-tight container, approximately 20 by 20 inches and 5 to 6 inches deep (We usually use a plastic bin or a large roasting pan.)
- Water
- Large spoon
- Fiberglass window screen, 10 by 10 inches
- Two ¼-inch wooden dowels, 10 inches long
- Duct tape
- Old kitchen towels or hand towels
- Baking sheets
- Scissors

Instructions

1. Have the children rip a bunch of paper into small pieces, the smaller the better.

2. Fill the container with about 3 inches of warm water.

3. Slowly add the bits of paper—give the kids a chance to mix it into the water. You want to add as much paper as possible while still maintaining a soupy mixture. Stop adding paper before the mixture starts looking like oatmeal.

4. Let the mixture sit overnight, so the paper has plenty of time to soak up water.

5. Meanwhile, tape the wooden dowels to opposite sides of the window screen. The dowels will serve as handles for the screen.

6. Now you're ready to make paper. Lay out your materials in this order: screen, container of drenched paper, a pair of folded towels.

7. Gently stir the water and paper mixture so there is plenty of paper suspended in the water—you don't want it all resting at the bottom of the container.

8. Pick up the screen by its handles and carefully slip it into the water mixture. The hand action is easier to do than explain—you're basically scooping a screen full of the mixture onto the screen. You want to evenly fill the screen with pulp and water. This is where practice comes in. Not enough pulp and your paper will be too thin to stick together. Too much pulp and you'll make cardboard. The wet pulp should be a bit thicker than you want your finished paper to be. You can push the paper around with your fingers to get it even if you like.

9. Patiently hold the screen over the container and let as much water as possible drain through the screen.

10. Carefully flip the screen over onto a towel. Place the second towel on top of the screen. The sandwich you have made should go like this: table, towel, paper pulp, screen, towel. Now, press down on the top towel to remove as much moisture as possible from the pulp.

11. Remove the top towel, and slowly peel up the screen so the pulp stays on the bottom towel.

12. After a few minutes, turn the bottom towel over on the baking sheet and gently peel the towel off, so the new piece of paper rests on the baking sheet.

13. Repeat until your baking sheets are filled with wet paper or until the kids get bored.

14. Let the paper dry—it might take a few days.

15. Use the scissors to trim up the edges of the paper if you like.

Variations

- Sprinkle some glitter onto the wet paper before removing it from the screen.

- Cut tiny pieces of colored ribbon, flowers, or grass, and add them to the water and paper mixture.

- Use a blender to make the paper pulp.

- Try drying the paper in different locations—does it dry quicker on a sunny picnic table or in a dark basement?

- Use a hole punch and twine to bind the finished pages together for a book.

- What happens if you add food coloring to the mixture?

Telling Tall Tales

Ages: Infancy +

Ease of Construction

Description In our fast-paced, technology-centered world, we tend to forget the power of simple storytelling. But watch a child's eyes when you're telling a good story. They're engaged, curious, learning. You don't have to be an expert to pull this off. All you need is a willing audience and a bit of imagination. With practice, you'll soon become more comfortable with the process and will make up more exciting stories.

Learning Telling tall tales shows children how words convey meaning and paint mental pictures, nurtures their fertile imaginations, and builds vocabulary and language comprehension. It also creates a feeling of closeness and community with other people.

Materials

None

Instructions

1. If you don't have much experience making up stories, start by telling classic stories like "Goldilocks and the Three Bears" or "The Three Little Pigs." As you grow more comfortable with story time, begin to experiment with content: What happens if the wolf can't blow down the house of straw? What happens if the children you are telling the story to appear at the bears' house before Goldilocks does? What happens if Little Red Riding Hood's grandmother is abducted by aliens?

2. With practice, you will be telling stories that are completely your own in no time. Here are a few tips to help you along:

   - Add familiar people, places, and things to your stories. Children love to be made part of the adventure, especially if they can play the hero.

   - Start with reality and transition into fantasy. For example, start with kids playing in the yard and then add a unicorn, a magic carpet, or a talking squirrel.

   - Keep stories short at first; you will lose kids' attention if the story goes on too long. Your stories can get longer as their attention spans do.

   - Mix new and exotic words into the stories to expand their vocabularies.

   - Always leave them wanting more. If you stop a story right before lunch with the main character hanging off the edge of a cliff clutching a bag of gold in her teeth while angry chipmunks are tossing acorns at her, I promise your audience will be eager to hear more when lunch is over.

Variations

- Let the kids tell you stories.
- Create a group story by taking turns adding sentences.
- After a story, encourage the children to draw or paint their favorite scene.

When I was little, my dad told me that he used to be a pirate (arrr matey!) and my mom a princess (whatever noise a princess makes!). He said that my mom was his one true love and that he saved her from her evil father and they lived happily ever after.

Nowadays, he tells the pirate story to the child care kids. He also tells them stories about animals that live in our basement: a pet dinosaur, an alligator, and my magic color-changing dairy cows that can turn invisible. I've become a storyteller too, and I play along with my dad and add to the tales he tells.

It started out innocently enough. One of the children in our family child care looked at the little door on the wall of the coat closet and asked, "What's that?" I explained that it was the door to something called a laundry chute. "What's that?" I was asked. I then explained what a laundry chute was and answered all laundry chute–related questions that were tossed my way. After satisfying the kids' curiosity, I went on with my day without another thought of laundry or chutes.

Of course their curiosity was not satisfied; I was a big fool for even thinking such a thing. Items from the closet started mysteriously disappearing down the chute: "I can't find my glove." "Where is my backpack?" "Someone took my hat!" Explaining the concept of laundry chute only partially quelled their curiosity. They needed to experience laundry chute. I understood—and respected—this need, but after a few weeks of understanding I was growing tired of trudging to the basement to retrieve the objects. I had to find a way to end this cycle. I could have just nailed the door shut since we don't regularly use the chute, but I decided that would be too easy. I had no choice but to tell them about the dinosaur that lived in our basement.

To start with, I gathered the schoolagers and nonchalantly explained that I knew they had been dropping things down the chute and that it needed to stop because the germs on their hats, gloves, and mittens were making my baby triceratops sick, and besides she might chew up their things because she was teething.

"That can't be true," one child muttered.

"Sure it's true," I countered. "You know how you have to wash your hands to get rid of the germs so they don't make you sick? We'll my baby dinosaur has never been around those germs before and when they get dropped down the chute on your things she gets sick. Yesterday I had to clean up a huge dinosaur puke mess."

"No, I mean it can't be true that you have a baby triceratops in your basement. Dinosaurs have been extinct for millions of years!" the child retorted.

"Yeah, there are no real dinosaurs anymore, only pretend dinosaurs," another added.

"That's exactly what I used to think," I began. "When we found the egg, I had no idea it would hatch or that it would be a dinosaur. It's amazing." I went on to explain how Tasha, my wife, and I had been out hiking one weekend afternoon a few years back when we found the egg half buried in a hillside covered in lichen and moss. We decided to haul it home, clean it up, and get a better look.

"How did it hatch?" they asked in unison.

"Well, at first we didn't think it would hatch, but while we were cleaning the egg it moved a little bit. That's when Tasha decided she would build a nest out of blankets and sit on it until it hatched."

"How long did she have to sit there?"

"Only about six weeks," I dryly answered.

"Six weeks!" they squealed. "How could she do that?"

I gave details and answered the flood of questions:

- I brought Tasha food and when she had to go to the bathroom she put the egg on a heating pad.

- *They could not see the baby dino because her immune system was not able to handle human germs and we wanted to keep her safe.*

- *We wore special suits when we fed her and played with her so our germs would not hurt her.*

- *They did not make those suits in kid sizes.*

- *She was a plant eater, but since she was a baby we had to give her a bottle a few times a day too.*

- *She was able to live in our basement because it was huge; that is the way they made them 100 years ago when the house was built.*

- *Yes, I had to clean up lots of dinosaur poop, it did smell, and I had fallen in it.*

- *We had not named her yet, she thought Tasha was her mom and I was her dad, she liked to cuddle and rub her nose on my neck, her horns were kind of sharp, she was about 5 feet tall and weighed 1,200 pounds.*

- *I could not take her picture yet because the flash from the camera would scare her . . . maybe when she gets older.*

- *They could see her in thirty-five years when she was grown up and her immune system was strong.*

Over the next few days there were a few more questions from kids and interested parents; I happily answered them all with a smile. Nothing disappeared down the chute for over a week and there was a renewed interest in dinosaur toys, dinosaur books, and dramatic play involving dinosaurs. Every once in a while there was an inquiry into her well-being or a request to "Pleeeeeeeeeease!" meet her. Then one day Anna dropped her new black boots down the chute when she was supposed to be putting them on to go home.

"I'll go get them," I said. "I hope the dinosaur doesn't get to them first."

"We don't think you really have a dinosaur," she snipped as her friends looked on. Her mother stood by with a faint smile as I headed to the basement.

A few minutes later, I returned. My hand, lower arm, and one of Anna's new boots dripped with a slimy, thick, translucent goo that was speckled with sopping chunks of gunk. "Anna, she was chewing on one of your boots, but I got it away from her," I said. "They should be okay once we clean them off. I really wish you wouldn't drop things down there anymore!"

The children's eyes bugged out as they watched glop dribble from the boots. Anna was sure her new boots were ruined until a few swipes of a paper towel revealed they were fine. The kids were now all believers and each assured me they would not drop anything else down the chute—and they haven't. It's amazing what you can accomplish with a good story, some liquid laundry detergent, and a bit of debris from the dryer lint trap.

Encouraging
math and Logical Thinking

Real cows don't fit in purses.

—Phoebe, age 2½

Phoebe's words struck me as both obvious and fascinating. I have known cows do not fit in purses for a long time. However, this wonderful young child had just realized, as she stuffed black and white plastic cows into a play purse, the utter absurdity and illogicality of a real cow fitting in a purse. She had figured out that, while many play cows fit in the purse just fine, the geometry of a real cow would be impossible to stuff into the tiny confines of her purse. It is realizations like this, things that seem so obvious to us world-wise adults, that make up math and logical thinking for young children.

In their everyday play, children are busy building an understanding of concepts like large and small, here and there, up and down, big and little, more and less. They are realizing what one is and how it is different from two. While their bodies are in constant motion, fooling around with blocks, kitchen timers, and plastic cows, their minds are absorbing the building blocks for math and logical thinking. Through hands-on experiences, interaction, child-guided play, exploration, and discovery, children lay the foundation for these lifelong skills. The projects that follow will help you offer this opportunity to the children in your care.

Phoebe shared another revelation later that week: "Houses don't have ears!"
Profound.

Streamer Launchers

Ages: 3+

Ease of Construction

Description Streamer launchers are simply prettied-up rubber bands that you can send sailing into the air. They are very easy to make and children love to play with them. It might take a little while to figure out the mechanics of launching them, but they're fun whether they fly a foot or clear across a room.

Learning The launchers help children develop small-muscle skills and hand-eye coordination. The laws of motion, kinetic energy, and if/then thinking are also introduced through this activity.

Materials

- ☐ Flagging tape (a plastic ribbon used to mark stakes or hazards on building sites; available at your local home center)
- ☐ Scissors
- ☐ Large rubber band
- ☐ Small plastic cable tie (available at your local home center)

Instructions

1. Cut three or four pieces of flagging tape, each 15 to 20 inches long.

2. Stack the pieces, fold them in half, and hold them at the center point.

3. Use the cable tie to tightly attach the rubber band to the center point of the pieces of flagging tape.

4. Cut off the tail of the cable tie.

5. To launch, loop the rubber band over your index finger, pull back on the flagging tape tail, aim, and let go.

Variations

- Make your streamer launchers fancy by using different colored flagging tape. You can find it in pink, orange, and yellow at most home centers; on the Internet it is available in many more colors as well as polka-dot, checkerboard, and striped patterns.

- Challenge kids to fire their launchers into a laundry basket across the room.

- As their aim improves, have them fire their launchers through a hula-hoop that another child is holding.

- Encourage children to try changing their hands around if you notice them doing it the same way all the time. This will help them develop muscles in their nondominant hand.

I usually carry a few streamer launchers with me when I present at conferences, to entertain myself and give away. A while back, I received an e-mail from a provider named Kim and at the end of her message she reminded me that I had given a launcher to her school-age daughter, Jordan. She told me they had lots of fun with it and that Jordan had the thing hanging in her room.

In my reply, I asked if Jordan would be willing to waste a bit of her summer vacation writing about the launcher and our time at the conference together. Here is what Jordan had to say:

I went to a conference with my mom and met a very silly but interesting guy named Jeff. Jeff gave me a streamer that you could shoot at things and he had one too. He showed me how to use it by putting your finger in the rubber band part and pulling back on the streamers and watching it fly. He showed me that if you hit the metal vents in the ceiling it makes a tyanggggggg sound—it was COOL.

He also told me it would not get stuck up there in the vents, and guess what happened? HIS streamer got stuck.

When me and my mom got home, we thought of a lot of games you can play with it. One of the games that we have fun playing is Basket-Streamer. Basketball . . . Basket-Streamer. The only thing different is you set up two hula hoops to shoot the streamer through instead of using hoops. The catch is that you can only shoot from half-court. You pass the streamer by shooting it also.

It was fun!

I cannot wait for the next time I see Jeff.

I can't imagine what silly thing he will do.

One way to find out is to help test his new toys!

From: Jordan

I have to admit, there are probably streamer launchers hanging from light fixtures, vents, and ductwork in over a dozen hotels and conference centers that I've visited. Those things sure do fly.

I also want to thank Jordan and her mom for inventing basket-streamer. It just goes to show how versatile projects and materials that pass the Empty Box Test can be.

Baking Up Some Math Skills

Ages: 2+

Ease of Construction

Description Inviting children to assist in the kitchen is a great way to help them learn math and thinking skills. Plus, they enjoy being helpful and doing grown-up tasks. Part of me thought it might be best to describe a healthier baking option, but we all have birthdays so knowing how to make a cake is a valuable skill for any child.

Learning Through baking, children learn number and measurement concepts: how many eggs do we need? how much cooking oil? They also practice following directions, learn about the importance of the written word, and discover how cause-and-effect relationships work. Using tools and utensils in the kitchen builds small-muscle skills. Waiting for a cake to bake also teaches patience—it takes a long time when you're a preschooler.

Materials

☐ Mixing bowl

☐ Large spoon

☐ Cake mix

☐ Water

☐ Eggs

☐ Cooking oil

☐ Cake pan

☐ Oven

Instructions

1. It's best to prepare as much as possible before the children join in. Have your materials organized and create a game plan.

2. Keep your group of bakers as small as possible. This gives everyone a chance to help and besides, you can only fit so many people around a mixing bowl.

3. From here on out, follow the directions on your cake mix. The materials list given here is probably pretty accurate, but make adjustments as needed.

4. Don't forget to eat the cake!

Variations

■ Add candles to the finished cake to bring more math into the mix.

■ Let children help cut the cake and serve the pieces. They can also count the pieces, plates, forks, and napkins.

■ If cake baking is a success, look for more ways to involve the children in cooking. Try homemade cake, applesauce, or a spaghetti lunch from scratch.

Weighing Things over with Kitchen Scales

Ages: 2+

Ease of Construction

Description While the kids are waiting for their cake to bake, let them begin experimenting with an inexpensive kitchen tool. A kitchen scale helps children understand how to measure weight. This is another chance to step back and let the children play, explore, and discover on their own. Remember, you're a professional play technician. Your job is to set the stage for learning and then step out of the way and let it happen.

Learning Children will learn the basics of object weight. This, in turn, helps them understand concepts like heavy, light, bigger, and smaller. They will begin to grasp that just because an object is larger, it's not necessarily heavier. Using a kitchen scale will also help children in their ongoing effort to classify and organize the objects they encounter in their daily lives.

Materials

☐ Small kitchen scale

☐ Small toys and items the kids can weigh, such as blocks, cars, plastic dinosaurs, and spoons

Instructions

1. Show children how the scale works and give them some general guidelines for using it properly.

2. Provide some materials (like the ones listed above) for them to weigh.

3. Step back and let them explore and make discoveries.

4. Be nearby to answer questions and intervene when needed. Remember, "I don't know" is a perfectly good answer sometimes. Just be sure to follow it up with something like "Let's see if we can find an answer."

Variations

▪ Try placing a small watertight container on the scale and weigh water, sugar, flour, or salt. Introduce measuring spoons so kids can begin measuring these substances two ways: by weight and by volume.

▪ Challenge older children to graph and chart the weights of items. For example, which weighs more, a cup of flour or a cup of water?

▪ Let them use the scale in their dramatic play. Provide paper and pencils so they can document their scale readings. The scale will quickly become part of an imaginary grocery store, science lab, or pediatrician's office.

▪ Try other types of scales. Bathroom scales and postage scales are easy to find and would be a fun variation.

Passing Time with Kitchen Timers

Ages: 2+

Ease of Construction

Description "There are only two long sleeps and two naps until my birthday!" a child chimes. Learning to understand the concept of time is a long and challenging task of childhood. This activity will give kids a chance to play with time and begin incorporating it into their world.

Learning This project is all about learning to understand and measure the passage of time, but children will also learn number identification, develop small-muscle skills, practice social skills, and hone communication skills.

Materials

☐ Inexpensive kitchen timer

Instructions

1. Show a few children how the timer works.

2. Step back and let them make it a part of their play. They will quickly figure out ways to integrate it into their favorite play scenarios, or they will invent brand-new ways to play.

3. Be there to support them, as needed.

Variations

■ Demonstrate how they can use the timer to see who can jump the most times in two minutes or stand on one foot for two minutes.

■ Use the timer to alert kids that a transition is coming. For example, set the timer for five minutes and tell them that when it sounds, it will be time to pick up toys for lunch.

■ Use the timer to help kids learn to share—"Okay, Monique, you can play at the light table until the timer sounds, then it is Bubba's turn."

The Scrap-Stack Game

Ages: 3+

Ease of Construction

Description I created this game to make use of all the wood scraps that somehow kept accumulating in my woodworking shop. Kids love it because it is challenging, competitive, and fun. They also love the inevitable *crash* that comes at the end of every match.

Learning Players will develop spatial relations skills, hand-eye coordination, cause-and-effect thinking, logical thinking, and creative thinking. They will also get to practice taking turns and using other social and language skills.

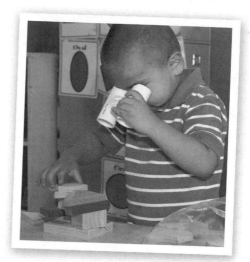

Materials

- ☐ Odd-shaped small wood scraps, around thirty of them (Pieces should not be smaller than 1-inch cubes or larger than 3-inch cubes.)
- ☐ Wooden base, ¾ inch thick and around 5 inches square
- ☐ Sandpaper

Instructions

1. Smooth out any rough or sharp edges on the pieces and the base with sandpaper. Kids love to help with this part of the project.
2. To play, each player takes a turn adding a piece to the base. The player who makes the stack crash loses.

Variations

- ▪ Hold a scrap-stack tournament.
- ▪ Make it more challenging by placing a playing piece under one edge of the base so the playing surface is uneven.
- ▪ Let players choose their opponents' playing pieces.
- ▪ If you really want a challenge, play in a canoe.
- ▪ Have older children use their nondominant hand. This will help strengthen that hand and improve coordination.

Milk Jug Lid Beading Set

Ages: 1+

Ease of Construction

Description Providing child care means that sometimes we have four kinds of milk plus orange juice or lemonade in our refrigerator. That is why it was so easy to convince the kids that we have dairy cows in our basement. At one time we had approximately 2.5 million lids from the gallon jugs of milk and juice that the children in our care had consumed over the years. Okay, maybe I exaggerate a little bit. Anyway, we had to do something with them and since our daughter, Zoë, had just received her own cordless drill as a gift, we decided to make the lids into beads. She went to work with her drill and in no time we had a collection of colorful, durable, and inexpensive beads to use.

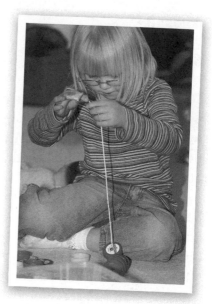

Learning Children will improve their small-muscle skills and hand-eye coordination as they string these beads. In addition, older children will develop sequencing, pattern recognition, color recognition, and counting skills.

Materials

- ☐ Drill with ¼-inch bit
- ☐ A bunch of milk jug lids, the more colors the better
- ☐ Nylon twine
- ☐ Scissors
- ☐ Duct tape

Instructions

1. Use the drill to carefully make a hole in the center of each lid. If you're uncomfortable with power tools, find someone to do this step for you. Holding the lid with a pair of channel-lock pliers will help keep it steady while you drill. Use a slow speed.

2. Cut a short length of nylon twine. We generally start with a piece around 16 inches long.

3. Use a small piece of duct tape to create a "needle" on one end of the twine. Just twist the tape around the top inch or so of the string so that the string will not fray.

4. Securely knot the other end of the twine to prevent beads from slipping off.

5. Show the kids how to string beads and then let them play.

SAFETY NOTE *Milk jug lids are pretty big, but if a child in your care finds a way to stick everything in his or her mouth, hold off on using this activity with that child. Most children eventually stop mouthing everything. Close supervision is, of course, a necessary part of working with any young child.*

Variations

- Create a pattern on one string and challenge children to repeat it on another string.

- String a bunch of lids onto a piece of twine and secure both ends to create a milk lid "snake." We made a green snake and a pink snake that the older children have used in dramatic play and that the toddlers and infants love to drag around the house.

- String the beads onto other things such as stiff wire or drinking straws.

- Let the children make their own colorful necklaces to take home. You can always make more beads, because they'll keep drinking milk.

- Challenge experienced beaders to add beads with their nondominant hand.

ZOË SAYS

Power tools are nothing to be afraid of. Some people are scared of these tools because they have never used them. But, they're just machines to help you complete tasks. Some people still think it is weird for girls to use power tools. That's so wrong. I mean, I've had a cordless drill for years. I asked for one for Christmas when I was nine. It made my dad so happy I think he cried a little. I also know how to use a scroll saw and lots of other power tools.

Then again, if you really feel uncomfortable using power tools, you can always find someone who's willing to do it for you.

watching Time fly

Ages: 2+

Ease of Construction

Description Here is another activity that helps familiarize children with the concept of time and numbers. All you need are a few inexpensive children's watches. You don't want to send the kids off to play with $250,000 watches made by Patek Philippe or Girard-Perregaux. Something plastic with a cartoon character on it will work just fine.

Learning Children will learn about the concept of time, identify numbers, and increase their numerical literacy. Playing with the watches is bound to increase their small-muscle skills as well.

Materials

☐ Inexpensive wristwatches

Instructions

1. Strap watches on tiny wrists.

2. Stand back.

3. Answer questions as they come up.

Variations

■ Even the most inexpensive digital watches usually come with a stopwatch function. Show children how to use this function in different games, like races or jump roping contests.

■ Help children understand the passage of time. Write down the time you will eat snack or go outside to play, and ask them to keep an eye on their watches and let you know when the proper time arrives.

■ Show older children how to find their pulse on their neck and count how many times their heart beats in a minute. Now have them run for a few minutes and check their pulse again. Discuss why their pulse changed after exercising.

Container and Lid Match

Ages: Infancy to 4

Ease of Construction

Description In addition to milk jug lids, we also have a warehouse full of yogurt, butter, sour cream, shampoo, ketchup, mouthwash, barbeque sauce, peanut butter, maple syrup, and other plastic containers. We keep an ever-changing selection of these containers and their lids in our playroom, and the children use them in a variety of ways.

Sometimes Sam inverts an empty barbeque sauce container, shakes it, and says, with a devilish grin, "I'm making a mess." He proceeds to pretend to pour barbeque sauce all over the floor, toys, and himself. Then he smiles and shouts "I'll clean it up," as he grabs a play dishcloth and cleans up the nonexistent mess.

Sometimes I pretend to drink from an empty bottle of shampoo just so Phoebe will rush over and scold me. "Jeffie, we don't drink shampoo," she says as she grabs my chin and nose and tries to pry my mouth open. "Spit it out or you'll get sick!"

Lots of learning can be done with these readily available materials. This lid matching game is something the kids invented and enjoy playing.

Learning It may look like they are simply putting lids on containers, but when small children do this they are learning about spatial relations, geometry, and physics as well as developing their hand-eye coordination, memory, small-muscle skills, and problem-solving abilities.

Materials

☐ Assorted empty and clean plastic containers and lids

Instructions

1. Stick the containers, with their lids on, someplace in your play environment for the children to find.

2. Stand back, let them discover the containers, and observe.

3. You will probably be called on to help remove some lids if children do not have much experience with the materials.

4. After they have some hands-on practice with the containers and lids, remove all the lids and see if they can put them back on the correct containers. This can be done one-on-one or with a small group of children working together.

Variations

■ Get out those cheap wristwatches and time older children as they match the lids. Have them chart their times and see how their time varies when they each have three or four chances to compete.

■ Hide blocks and other toys in containers for infants and toddlers to find when they remove the lids.

■ Use the containers like blocks to build towers and castles.

■ Add these containers to your dramatic-play or water-play area.

■ Scents may linger in the containers. Have children close their eyes and see if they can guess what used to be in a container you hold up to their noses.

frameless wooden Puzzles

Ages: 1+

Ease of Construction

Description We wanted some puzzles that had only two or three pieces and would stand up to the wear and tear of busy and curious toddlers. We could not find any that met our needs, so we started making our own. These puzzles have just a few easy-to-manipulate pieces and are made from cabinet-grade plywood, so they will stand up to years of play.

Learning Children will learn geometric thinking, spatial relations, hand-eye coordination, problem solving, and thinking skills while they put these puzzles together. They will also be developing small-muscle skills.

Materials

- ☐ Puzzle template (See pages 117–121.)
- ☐ ¾-inch cabinet-grade plywood
- ☐ Masking tape
- ☐ Sandpaper
- ☐ Scroll saw or band saw
- ☐ Dust rag

Instructions

1. Copy one of the templates on pages 117–121 or find one of your own.
2. Tape the template to the plywood.
3. Use a scroll saw or band saw to cut out the animal shape.
4. Reattach the template and cut the animal shape into pieces, as shown on the template.
5. Sand the pieces well and gently round over all edges.
6. Wipe the pieces clean with a dry rag.
7. Let the children put the finished puzzles together.

Variations

- Mix the pieces of two or three puzzles together and challenge a child to reassemble them.
- Allow children to paint the puzzles. (Make sure you use child-safe paint.)
- Laminate three pieces of plywood together and follow the directions above to create animal puzzles that can stand on their own legs.

Where Will It Go When You Blow?

Ages: 2+

Ease of Construction

Description There, behind the loveseat! Is it a sly warrior with a blowgun and a poison-tipped arrow, or is it a four-year-old with a drinking straw and a cotton swab? You decide. With this activity, kids get a chance to fire projectiles across the room. What could be more fun?

Learning Logical thinking, problem solving, and physics are all part of this activity. Kids will also learn about measuring and numbers and develop hand-eye coordination.

Materials

- ☐ Drinking straws
- ☐ Cotton swabs
- ☐ Small bucket or tote
- ☐ Tape measure
- ☐ Masking tape

Instructions

1. Put a cotton swab into one end of a drinking straw.

2. Blow into the other end of the straw.

3. After practicing by yourself for a while, show the children how to do steps 1 and 2.

4. Place the bucket or tote on the floor.

5. Have the children measure 3, 5, 8, and 10 feet from the container and place a piece of tape on the floor at each location.

6. Let everyone fire a cotton swab from each line and record who fires into the container from each spot.

Variations

- ■ Have older children add up the distance of all the shots they made and then chart the results.

- ■ Hang a hula hoop from a tree branch and blow cotton swabs through the hoop. Now try doing it while the hoop is swinging.

- ■ See who can launch the most cotton swabs into the container in a minute and graph the results of each child.

SAFETY NOTE *We've never experienced any problems with this activity. Nonetheless, make sure kids know to blow and not suck on the straw with the cotton swab in it. The chance of getting hit in the eye is small, but kids should be encouraged not to aim for anyone's face. Monitor the activity closely.*

Bucket Cable Car

Ages: 3+

Ease of Construction

Description The seed for this project was planted in my head years ago when Zoë and some other kids built a cable car for a bunch of Barbie dolls who wanted to go skiing. Using yarn, drinking straws, lots of tape, and a cardboard box, they spent hours refining their design and hauling the dolls to the slopes. This project is just a heavy-duty version of their creation.

Learning Understanding how this rig works takes a lot of logical thinking. Kids will also develop their small- and large-muscle skills, use their imaginations, and gain a better understanding of gravity, motion, energy, and other aspects of physical science.

Materials

- ☐ Plastic bucket
- ☐ Duct tape
- ☐ ½-inch PVC pipe, 8 inches long
- ☐ ¼-inch rope
- ☐ Cable ties
- ☐ Nylon twine

Instructions

1. Securely tape the piece of PVC to the bucket handle.

2. Determine where your cable car will run and what you will anchor it to. A good choice is in the yard between two trees. You want the children to be able to reach the rope on at least one side.

3. Thread the PVC pipe onto the ¼-inch rope and string the rope between the two points. Tie it off so that the rope is tight and suspended above the ground like a clothesline.

4. Loosely attach a cable tie at each end of the rope to create loops. The nylon twine will pass through these loops and allow the cable car to move along the ¼-inch rope.

5. On the left side of the bucket, tie an end of the nylon twine to the point where the handle meets the bucket.

6. Run the twine to the left, following the rope, and through the left cable tie loop.

7. Then run the twine back to the right, thread it through the PVC pipe, then through the right cable tie loop.

8. Bring the twine back to the bucket. Pull it taut and tie it to the point on the right side of the bucket where the handle meets the bucket. (See the illustration on page 43.)

9. Now, standing in one place and pulling on the nylon twine should make the bucket move along the ¼-inch rope.

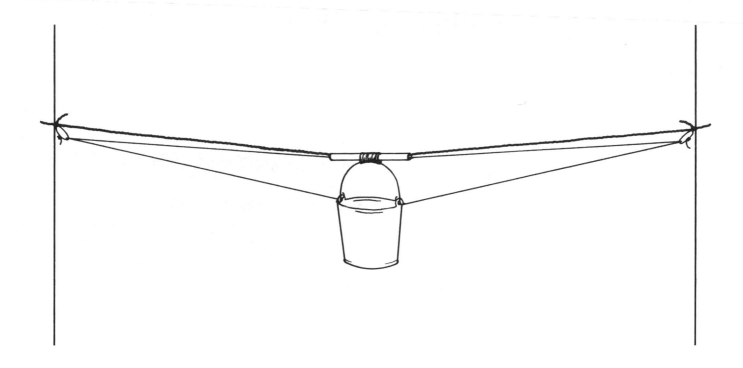

Variations

■ Make one end of the rope higher than the other. At our house we have it run between two hooks, one anchored low on a wall and the other in the ceiling. The bucket climbs about 7 feet as it moves from one end of the room to the other.

■ The second time you put together this apparatus, let the kids do all the work. It will test their memory and allow them to do some thinking and problem solving.

■ Install the cable car in different locations each time you put it up to add variety to the play.

■ Have the kids haul a variety of toys and materials in the bucket—stuffed animals, small dolls, and so on.

Critter Trap

Ages: 3+

Ease of Construction

Description My child care buddy Pam in Sioux Falls, South Dakota, sent me a picture of the children in her family child care program trying to trap gophers with an apparatus similar to the one described here. It looked like so much fun, I had to share her great idea. The odds of kids actually catching something aren't really high, but it should keep them quiet and entertained for a good long time.

Learning During this activity, children will learn if/then thinking: *if* they lie on the ground long enough and be quiet enough, and *if* they use the right bait, and *if* they pull the string fast enough, *then* they will catch a critter. They will learn hand-eye coordination. They will learn patience. They will learn it can be a ton of fun hanging around outside trying to get close to nature.

Materials

☐ Nylon twine, 10 to 20 feet long

☐ A stick, around a foot long

☐ Plastic laundry basket

☐ Bait

Instructions

1. Tie one end of the nylon twine to the stick.

2. Turn the basket upside down someplace in your yard.

3. Prop up one end of the basket with the stick.

4. Put the bait under the basket. If you really want the kids to catch something, use bait that critters in your part of the world like to eat. If you don't want them to catch anything, use something like cauliflower or licorice.

5. Carefully stretch out the twine.

6. Explain to the kids that they need to lie on the ground quietly and wait until a bird, rabbit, squirrel, armadillo, or bobcat walks under the basket to eat the bait. Tell them that once a critter is under the basket, they need to pull the twine real fast so the basket falls on it. Then they need to run and sit on the basket so whatever they caught doesn't escape.

7. Watch from a distance with a smile on your face.

Variation

■ To keep them at it longer, offer a bounty for every critter they catch—maybe $3 for each bird, $5 for each rabbit or squirrel, $10 for raccoons, and $100 for a wolf or elk. Make sure they have paper and pens so they can make a list of how they will spend all their money.

Exploring
Science and Problem Solving

Jeff, please *don't touch it. I need to look at it tomorrow!*

—Jack, age 5, after discovering a dead bird writhing with bugs
and maggots in my yard while on his way to his mom's car

Does Darth Vader poop?

—Sam, 2½, as he battles constipation

This chapter provides activities that will allow children to practice being scientists and hone their observational skills. The activities encourage them to ask questions and search for answers. Children are natural explorers and eager to understand the world they live in, yet many of us caregivers are scared of science. It is my hope that these projects will engage the children and not scare you off. The best way for us adults to promote science with preschoolers is to get over any fears or bad memories from our own school years and play, explore, and discover. Sometimes preschool science is messy and icky, but we can handle that; after all, we work with kids every day.

As for the quotes above, I did leave the dead bird where it was for Jack to investigate the next day. I also sat and watched the writhing white maggots for quite a while after he heeded his mother's calls and climbed into the car. The answer to Sam's question has to be yes, and I bet the smell is powerful.

Now, I have some schoolagers waiting to go on an adventure to interact with nature at the state park down the road. We're going to turn over rocks, hunt for bugs, look at dead stuff if we find it, watch plants, and practice being scientists. These are some of the same things you can do with the activities that follow. Keep reading; I have to go.

Elastic Sound Waves

Ages: 3+

Ease of Construction

Description In this activity, a small length of elastic is used to play with sound waves. One thing many adults may see as a big plus for this activity is that to participate, children need to spend a few minutes quiet and still.

Learning Children will begin to understand that sound is made by vibrations that send waves traveling through the air to our ears. They will also hone their small-muscle skills and hand-eye coordination.

Materials

- ¼-inch elastic
- ¾-inch elastic
- Scissors

Instructions

1. Cut a length of both widths of elastic for each child; make them about 8 to 12 inches long. There is no need to measure precisely.

2. Have the children place their hands gently on their throats and then have them hum.

3. Explain that the vibrations they feel in their hands are made by air moving a group of little bands in their voice boxes and that when those bands vibrate, sound is made. You can also talk about guitar or violin strings, or the vibrations a drumhead makes when you strike it.

4. Have each child hold a piece of elastic between the thumb and middle finger of one hand. Show them how the elastic can be stretched and retracted by moving their fingers in and out.

5. Holding the elastic in front of them, have the children strum the elastic with one of their index fingers. Ask if they hear anything.

6. Now, have them position the elastic near their ears and strum some more. Explain that if they change the length of the elastic, the sound will also change.

7. Let them try the other width of elastic and see if they note any differences.

8. Allow as much time as they need to explore.

Variations

- Infants and toddlers can't manage the elastic by themselves, but you can hold one to their ears and do the strumming for them. The curious look they will probably give you is priceless.

- Allow the children to personalize their elastic bands with markers.

- Make sure they show their parents that they learned how to make sound waves.

- Challenge them to find other materials that vibrate and make sound.

fizz-fizz-pop

Ages: 3+

Ease of Construction

Description Young children rarely need antacid tablets for their intended purpose, so why not use them for some science fun? In this project, young scientists discover that the gas bubbles made by an antacid tablet and a bit of water can launch a film canister lid into the air.

Learning This project will expose children to basic chemistry as they witness the amazing reaction between water and antacid tablets. They will also learn to make a prediction and then test that prediction in a controlled way—this is the basis for all modern science.

Materials

- ☐ Transparent cup
- ☐ Antacid tablets
- ☐ Paper and pen
- ☐ Teaspoon
- ☐ Water
- ☐ Empty 35 mm film canister (Clear containers work better, but the black ones with gray lids will do.)
- ☐ Towel

Instructions

1. Fill the cup about half full of water.

2. Gather the children and show them an antacid tablet and the cup of water.

3. Ask them to predict what will happen when the tablet is dropped into the water. Record their predictions. Let one of the children drop a tablet into the water.

4. Discuss what happens and refer to their predictions to see if anyone guessed correctly.

5. Now ask them what they think would happen if they placed the water and tablet into a small container with a tight-fitting lid. Again, record their predictions.

6. Put a teaspoon of water into the film canister.

7. Have the children take a few steps back. Drop the tablet into the canister and quickly secure the lid, place the canister on the table, and step back.

8. Wait. In a few seconds, the gas produced by the water and tablet should blow the lid off the canister. If it doesn't happen within thirty seconds, the canister lid probably is not on tight enough.

9. Repeat steps 6–8 as many times as you like. We can usually get a few launches out of one tablet simply by adding a bit more water. Allow the children to perform the experiment themselves. After a while, the canisters and lids do not seal as well as they did at first. If you start experiencing misfires, it might be time to start using a new canister.

10. Discuss the predictions they made in step 5.

11. Grab a towel and clean up.

Variations

■ Kids younger than three will love to watch this experiment even if they don't understand everything that is going on.

■ Experiment with different amounts of water, number of tablets, water temperature, or containers. Record your findings and see which methods work best.

■ Try to coordinate multiple launches by adding a few more film canisters to the mix. One flying film canister lid is fun; half a dozen is a real blast.

■ Get out those wristwatches again and time how long it takes for the canister lids to blow.

SAFETY NOTE *It probably goes without saying, but kids should stand back during this activity and there should always be adult supervision.*

Go toward the Light

Ages: Infancy to 3

Ease of Construction

Description Our chocolate lab, Chewy, loved to chase the red spot of a keychain laser light up and down the hall—the rug bunching up under her scampering feet, just like in the cartoons. Then I figured that if it was fun for the dog, why not try it with some infants and toddlers? They had the same reaction—a mix of fascination and curiosity. One child we cared for would try to gently pick up the light from the floor. We also taught her that if she blew on the light, it would magically disappear.

Learning This use of a laser is a good way to feed the curiosity of young children. That curiosity is going to lead to attempts to understand the light, where it is coming from, why and how it moves, and how it works. The children will become scientists trying to understand a new phenomenon. Chasing the laser light around the room will also challenge their small and large muscles, hand-eye coordination, and advanced thinking skills.

Materials

☐ Keychain laser

Instructions

1. Simply aim the light on the floor or walls where a child will spot it. Then move it or turn it off as the child moves in for closer analysis.

SAFETY NOTE *To avoid eye damage, never shine the light into a child's face, and avoid shining it into highly reflective surfaces.*

Variations

■ Darken the room to make the light more visible.

■ Give toddlers small, clear containers and see if they can "catch" the dot of light with the container.

■ Let older children run the laser light show. Make sure they follow safety rules.

wonderful wiggly worms of science

Ages: 2+

Ease of Construction

Description Whether it is hands-on or from a distance, most children are very curious about worms. This activity gives kids a chance to get as up close and personal with worms as they choose. If they want to feel the creepy critters wiggling in their fingers, that's fine. If they would rather observe from a distance, they can.

Learning Kids will learn to respectfully interact with nature and practice using their powers of observation—both very important skills for young scientists. This activity also allows children to use all their senses to more deeply understand another living creature.

Materials

- ☐ Earthworms
- ☐ Plastic storage container, 5 to 6 liters
- ☐ Soil from the ground or potting soil
- ☐ Paper and pencils

Instructions

1. Unless you happen to have a supply of earthworms, purchase some from the sporting goods department of your local big-box store or a bait store.

2. Add some moist, not wet, soil to your plastic container.

3. Let the kids set the worms in the container.

4. Observe the worms as they wiggle and tunnel into the soil.

5. Have the children draw or write about what they observe.

6. Make sure the children who want to handle the worms are allowed to do so. Discuss how to handle them gently. Hands should be washed before and after touching the worms.

7. When you're all done watching the worms, donate them to your favorite fisherman or, better yet, return them to the store for a refund. Tell the customer service clerk the worms were afraid of the water and that made them useless for fishing.

Variations

- If you would like to keep the worms around for a few days, use a nontranslucent container—worms like darkness. You will also need to drill or poke some holes around the upper edge of the container so the soil becomes oxygenated. Moist pet food will work as food, but you can also toss them a few table scraps. Store the container in a dark, cool place.

- Race the worms! Cut a piece of string or yarn 3 or 4 feet long, and tie the ends together. Spray down a shady patch of concrete with a hose and then lay the string out in the shape of a circle. Now let the kids each pick their favorite worm and place it in the center of the circle. The first worm to wiggle out of the ring is the winner!

- Check out a bait shop for mealworms, caterpillars, leeches, crickets, and different kinds of worms. If you don't have a bait shop nearby, shop online and they'll ship live critters right to your door.

mixing oil and water

Ages: 2+

Ease of Construction

Description This is another chance for children to practice being scientists. They will be mixing oil and water together and observing what happens. It's very simple, but that's the point: early learning doesn't have to be complicated. Kids will be happy to have a chance to pour and stir stuff together; science just kind of sneaks in the back door.

Learning Children will learn to make predictions and revise those predictions based on their observations. They will improve their observational skills. If they get to pour and stir, they will work on their small-muscle skills and hand-eye coordination. They will also be developing their language skills as they chatter away.

Materials

☐ Plastic container, small and clear

☐ Water

☐ Food coloring

☐ Craft stick

☐ Vegetable oil

Instructions

1. Pour some water into the container, add a few drops of food coloring, and mix with a craft stick.

2. Add some vegetable oil. Before pouring, ask the children to predict what will happen when you add the oil.

3. Stir the liquids together. Let them settle, and see what happens.

4. Repeat step 3 as many times as the kids want.

5. Discuss what you have observed and encourage the children to create a hypothesis based on what they observe.

Variations

■ Experiment with different amounts of each liquid.

■ Let the children dip a finger in the vegetable oil and taste it.

■ If you want the oil to mix with the water, simply add a few drops of dish soap.

■ Add some dark corn syrup to the mixture. Before adding it, ask children to predict whether it will sink or float.

■ To create a neat sensory bottle, pour some oil and water into a small plastic water bottle and hot-glue or duct-tape the lid on. You can also add some food coloring, glitter, or small craft items to the bottle before sealing it up.

Attracting Creepy-Crawlies

Ages: 2+

Ease of Construction

Description A lot of people spend piles of money every year to rid their yards of bugs, but some of us like to create comfy homes for them. Here is a simple way to encourage some nonpesky creepy-crawlies to move into your yard for the children to discover.

Learning Children will learn about the natural world around them and gain an appreciation for the diversity of life. They will learn to be good observers and to be thoughtful about how they interact with nature. This is yet another chance for children to practice being scientists.

Materials

☐ Cement paving stones, various sizes

☐ Water

☐ Notebook and pen

Instructions

1. Find an out-of-the-way location in your yard in which to create your bug and worm habitat. Look for a spot that is not too sunny, has good drainage, and is easily accessible.

2. Wet the ground and allow the water to soak in.

3. With the help of the children, place the cement pavers on the ground.

4. In your notebook, write "Bug Attracting Project" or "Operation Insect." Record the date and any other information the children feel might be important.

5. Wait a week, and check under the pavers. Record the date, and note any changes to the ground under the paver. If the ground is very dry, moisten it again. Replace the paver.

6. Repeat step 5 once a week for as long as the children are interested. Record your findings. It may take some time, but eventually you will begin to find signs of life under the paver.

Variations

■ Encourage the children to draw or write about critters they find under the pavers.

■ Make an open-face peanut butter and jelly sandwich. Place it in a disposable pie pan. Place the pan on the ground. Wait for bugs. Have the children suggest other things bugs might want to eat and try those items. Keep a log of what the bugs like to eat and what they stay away from.

■ Instead of pavers, set out large pieces of wood around the yard that the children can turn over to search for bugs.

Build an Arthropod Observation and Containment Unit

Ages: Infancy +

Ease of Construction

Description Arthropod Observation and Containment Unit—it sure sounds impressive. Well, what we're really talking about is a see-through container for the scientific study and examination of insects. Okay, what we are *really* talking about is a plastic baby food container with some holes punched in the lid for watching bugs. Call it what you want, kids love them.

Learning This project will help children sharpen their observational skills and gain respect for nature. It will also help them develop hand-eye coordination, small- and large-muscle skills, and a sense of connectedness to their environment.

Materials

☐ Plastic baby food containers and lids

☐ Pointed scissors or knife

Instructions

1. *Carefully* punch a few tiny slits in the lids with the scissors or a knife.

2. Give the children the containers and lids and send them outside to catch some bugs.

3. After they are done looking at their subjects, make sure they release the bugs back into their natural habitat. Explain that scientists like to study other creatures, but that it is always good to let them go back to their homes.

Variations

■ Use the containers to set up a bug zoo for parents or other adults to visit.

■ Encourage the children to draw, write, and tell stories about their bugs and the adventures they had while capturing them.

■ Don't make this a onetime activity. Have a supply of Arthropod Observation and Containment Units handy at all times for the little scientists in your life to use when needed.

ZOË SAYS

Have you ever been on a walk with a kid and they found a cool-shaped rock that they just had to keep? That happened to me a lot when I was little, so I came up with a way I could carry more stuff without weighing down my dad. I made a custom walking stick. All I had to do was grab a long hunk of wood from my dad's shop and attach an ice-cream bucket to it. Then as we hiked, I could just add my treasures to the bucket. Man, the things I used to collect. I remember one time I picked up dried fish heads we found along a river trail. Yes, I said dried fish heads.

Pumping Up Water Play

Ages: 1+

Ease of Construction

Description This project helps children delve into the applied science of fluid dynamics, the study of how liquids and gasses move. It sounds fancy, but what we're really going to be doing is using the pump from a lotion or liquid soap bottle to move water around. It's simple, hands-on, and wet—all the makings for a fun time.

Learning Here is another activity that helps kids sharpen their observational skills and learn more about how the world works. It is important to remember that many experiences are new to young children. Because they are looking at the world with fresh eyes, we have to make sure they have the time they need to fully explore objects and ideas. Through this water play, they will also learn about using tools, explore the properties of water, and improve muscle skills.

Materials

- ☐ Pump tops from lotion and liquid soap containers
- ☐ Water
- ☐ Scissors
- ☐ Sink, plastic tote, or water-play table

Instructions

1. Make sure the pumps you have salvaged are clean. Pumping warm soapy water through them will do the job.

2. You may want to trim the intake tube on some longer pumps. This makes them easier for children to handle and helps keep the water in the sink and off the floor.

3. Set up for water play.

4. Demonstrate how to use the pumps.

5. Let the kids explore the pumps, and be available to answer questions or assist as needed.

Variations

- ▪ Put some water and food coloring in a cup and pump it out into the water-play table.
- ▪ Try pumping chocolate pudding.
- ▪ Encourage children to use the pumps with their nondominant hand.

Passing Gas in the Kitchen

Ages: 3+

Ease of Construction

Description The passing of gas in this project will be done by baker's yeast (*Saccharomyces cerevisiae*), a one-celled fungus that breaks down sugar and starch and turns it into carbon dioxide bubbles and alcohol. These little critters hang around, eat, and then, uh, well they pass gas—a lot like humans. Unlike human gas, yeast gas is not very offensive smelling and is actually useful. It's in our bread, beer, and wine.

In this activity we're simply going to give some yeast a warm place to live and a good meal so we can watch them grow (and pass gas).

Learning Kids will learn that all living things need a source of energy and have certain conditions in which they thrive. This is also a chance to learn about the diversity of life and following directions.

Materials

- [ ] Pen and masking tape
- [ ] Four cereal bowls
- [ ] Measuring cup
- [ ] Measuring spoons
- [ ] Warm water (between 115 and 125 degrees Fahrenheit)
- [ ] Spoon
- [ ] Baker's yeast, three packages
- [ ] Sugar

Instructions

1. As you go through the following steps, label each bowl with the ingredients it will contain.

2. Pour 1 cup of warm water into the first bowl.

3. In the second bowl, mix 1 cup warm water and a packet of yeast.

4. In the third bowl, mix 1 tablespoon of sugar and a packet of yeast.

5. In the fourth bowl, mix 1 tablespoon of sugar and a packet of yeast, and then add this dry mixture to the cup of warm water in the first bowl.

6. Observe the bowls for a while and note any changes (or lack of changes). Keep checking back throughout the day and see if anything has happened.

ZOË SAYS

One morning when I went down to the kitchen for breakfast, there sitting on the counter was a bowl of yeast, sugar, and water. Dad was experimenting again. Every once in a while it would bubble like the purple goop in Ghostbusters. *When I came down later, the yeast was in a bigger bowl and still bubbling. Every time I went into the kitchen that day, the yeast was in a bigger container and bubbling more and more.*

The next day, my dad was leaning over a kids' swimming pool full of bubbling yeast with a big smile on his face when all of the sudden a really big bubble popped right in his face. It was hilarious. I almost suffocated to death from laughing so hard. For some reason he didn't find it funny. My mom wasn't too happy with the mess, either.

Variations

- Have children draw pictures of a yeast cell eating and making gas.

- Make sure everyone gets a chance to smell and taste the yeast.

- If some bowls do not have a reaction (they won't), ask the children to figure out what was missing from the bowl and add it.

- Try adding food coloring to the water, yeast, and sugar mixture.

- Try keeping your yeast as a pet and see how long you can keep it growing. You'll need to experiment with feeding it and keeping it warm. If you consider naming your pet yeast, keep in mind that there are millions of individual cells that will need naming, so keep a baby name book handy.

- Put the warm water, yeast, and sugar mixture in a yogurt or butter container. Put on the lid. Wait. If the lid fits well, it should pop off the container as the gas builds up inside—just like the antacid tablets earlier in this chapter (see pages 47–48).

- Show children a slice of bread and explain that the bubbles in the bread were made by yeast gas.

- Bake some homemade bread with the kids. If it looks good when it comes out of the oven and the kids all washed their hands really well before they started baking, send me a couple slices. The address is 1524 Summit Street, Sioux City, IA, 51103.

Build Your Own Museum of Oddities

You'll need a bigger container if you find a dead hippo or cow.

—Luke, age 5

Ages: 1+

Ease of Construction

Description It started innocently enough; when my kids were young we would go on walks and they would find fascinating stuff like pinecones, rocks, and leaves that they wanted to bring home. Then one of the moms at the center I directed starting working at a house-moving company. She spent a lot of time crawling around under old buildings, where she found neat stuff like the skulls of squirrels, opossums, and raccoons. Like a good mom, she brought them home for her sons to look at and they suggested bringing them to me. About this same time, someone brought me a fetal shark preserved in a jar of alcohol because they just knew the kids at the center would love to see it (they did). Then I started saving things like dead bats, birds, frogs, and baby squirrels in jars of alcohol. I'm even lucky enough to have a few genuine dinosaur bone fragments that a local bone hunter shared with me. Now, after sixteen years or so of collecting this weird stuff, I have quite an assortment.

Okay, I know a few people reading this are thinking I'm a gross, yucky, icky weirdo. I even considered leaving this section out of the book because I don't want you to think I'm a gross, yucky, icky weirdo, but in the end, I decided I could live with that sign around my neck—the way children react and interact with these artifacts is that remarkable. Look at the face of the child in this picture. She spent twenty minutes studying that baby squirrel. She counted its fingers and toes. She cradled it in her arms like a baby doll. She named it. Children study these things closely, bubble with questions, share insights, make connections, and they never call me gross, yucky, icky, or weird. They are intrigued by these oddities because they are innately curious and fascinated by the unknown.

I've also shared pieces of my collection with providers at conferences across the country and they generally have two reactions. Either they love the stuff and know the kids in their care would love it, or they cringe, grit their teeth, call me gross, and admit the children would love the stuff.

I'm going to share how we preserved the things in those jars. If this is too icky for you, skip to the next activity. I promise it won't be gross.

Learning Studying oddities like bison skulls, turtle shells, and a jar of squirrel helps children sharpen their observational skills and experience nature in a new, up-close way. This is hands-on early childhood science; kids are learning to make observations and ask questions about the world around them. They also learn to move carefully and use their small-muscle skills mindfully as they handle the items.

Materials

- [ ] Something to preserve
- [ ] Latex gloves
- [ ] Plastic bag
- [ ] Clear jars with tight-fitting, water-tight lids
- [ ] Rubbing alcohol
- [ ] Soap and warm water

Instructions

1. Locate the expired critter you want to preserve. There is no easy way to put this—freshness is important. You don't want anything that has been dead too long; decomposition is the enemy. Most of the exhibits in our museum of oddities were found by children during walks in the neighborhood. If you want to find something dead, go for a walk with a three-year-old.

2. Collect the specimen. I often take a pair of latex gloves and a plastic bag with me on walks.

3. Place the specimen in a clean jar.

4. Fill the jar with rubbing alcohol.

5. Secure the lid.

6. Throw away the gloves and bag and wash your hands with soap and warm water.

7. Let the children examine the specimen, as they are interested. Make sure they know it must be handled gently. It is a rule at our house that we *never* shake the jars or remove the lids. We only periodically make the specimens available for viewing; they are not something you want out all the time, and they should always be used under close supervision.

8. We usually change the alcohol after about six months. It tends to discolor during that time and the specimens just look better in crystal clear liquid. You may experience a new and interesting smell when you remove the lid to do this.

Variations

- If you're not interested in collecting your own specimens, ask a local high school or college science department if they have specimens that you could either bring the children to see or that they would be willing to bring to your program for a visit.

- Encourage children to draw or write about the critters you preserve.

- Over the last few years caregivers have shared delightful stories about taking children to visit butchers, seafood shops, landfills, and taxidermists to learn more about the natural world. Consider a similar outing of your own.

freezer Bag Science

Ages: 3+

Ease of Construction

Description This is an easy scientific experiment that involves coughing on slices of moist bread to see what will grow. Perhaps I was wrong when I wrote in the last activity that this one would not be gross. It *is* less gross than dead stuff in jars, and in any case, the kids will love it!

Learning Children will learn to conduct scientific experiments, hypothesize, develop their observation skills, and practice following directions.

Materials

☐ Freezer bags, 1-quart size

☐ Marker

☐ Paper and pen

☐ Bread

☐ Spray bottle of water

Instructions

1. For each child, label a bag with the child's name and the date.

2. Give each child a freezer bag and a slice of bread.

3. Explain that they are going to put some germs on the bread and see if they grow.

4. Let them take turns giving each slice of bread a squirt or two from the spray bottle. We want the bread to be moist, not wet.

5. Have them cough on their bread a few times.

6. Now, they should slip the bread into their bag and seal it.

7. Place the bags in a warm location out of direct sunlight.

8. Ask the children to predict what will happen to the bread and record their answers.

9. Check the bags in a week and see if they notice any changes. Let them update or revise their previous predictions.

10. Repeat step 9 for as long as the kids are interested.

11. Throw the bags away, unless the kids want to take them home to hang on their refrigerators.

Variations

■ Open the bag and smell.

■ Instead of coughing on the bread, let the kids gently wipe them across kitchen counters, doorknobs, shoe bottoms, or bathroom floors.

■ Try putting different stuff in bags—a cucumber, a taco, or maybe breakfast cereal. Check the bags every week or so and see what happens.

■ Put a serving of today's lunch in a plastic storage container and stick it in the back of the refrigerator. Check it regularly and see if it changes over time.

Them Bones, Them Bones, Them wonderful Bones

Ages: 2+

Ease of Construction

Description Children are fascinated by the natural world and will love the chance to look at and handle real bones. They will also enjoy observing and helping with the bone preparation process. Early science is all about observation and questions. The children I've shared my bone collection with spend lots of time looking them over and asking bone-related questions.

Learning Children will develop observational skills, increase their understanding of natural science, and practice asking science-related questions. They will also improve their language, small-muscle, and thinking skills.

Materials

☐ Large bones (We like turkey leg bones.)

☐ Stove

☐ Large saucepan or stockpot

☐ Boiling water

☐ White glue

☐ Container large enough to submerge bones

Instructions

1. Submerge bones in boiling water for 30 minutes and then leave them to soak overnight in warm water.

2. Remove any remaining meat and cartilage from the bones and rinse them thoroughly.

3. In the container, prepare an equal-part solution of water and white glue. Make enough of this mixture to completely cover the bones. This concoction will strengthen the bones and help preserve them.

4. Fully submerge the bones in the glue-water mixture and let them soak for 48 hours.

5. Let the bones dry completely. This may take a few days. A sunny windowsill is a great drying location.

6. Add the bones to your Museum of Oddities. Allow children to explore the bones.

Variations

■ Let the kids paint the bones.

■ Prepare two or more dry bones and let the kids use them as rhythm sticks.

■ Encourage children to hold a bone in one hand and then touch it to their opposite foot, knee, elbow, or shoulder.

ZOË SAYS

Well if you've ever known a kid, you probably know kids play with just about everything. It may seem odd to let them play with bones, but they play with their food, and tiny bits of string, and even their boogers. (Kids are weird, but I guess that's better than playing with someone else's boogers.) The thing is, they like to explore and learn about the world around them. It's important for them to play with a wide variety of objects—even the weird stuff.

Ice Cold Baby

Ages: Infancy to 2

Ease of Construction

Description It is easy to get caught up in the physical care of infants and toddlers and forget that they are busy scientists who need opportunities to explore their world. This is a simple activity that will stimulate their senses and minds. You can try it with older children too, but we wanted to include something sciencey just for this age group.

Learning This activity will encourage exploration, hand-eye coordination, and small-muscle activity. It will also offer a wide variety of sensory stimulation.

Materials

- ☐ Empty yogurt cups or similar-sized containers
- ☐ Water
- ☐ Juice
- ☐ Freezer
- ☐ Eating chair and tray

Instructions

1. Fill the containers with water or a juice-water mixture.
2. Freeze until solid.
3. Take the ice out of the containers and let it sit while you place a child in the chair with a selection of the cubes.
4. Talk to the child as he or she plays and explores.
5. Clean up as needed.

 *Always supervise children when they are playing with or eating food.*

Variations

- ■ For older infants and toddlers, add small pieces of food such as mashed banana, peas, or corn to the containers before freezing so the finished cubes will have more texture.
- ■ Place a plastic baby toy in a larger container (yogurt or butter), fill it with water, freeze, and let the child play. Leave part of the toy sticking out of the water so it can be used as a handle when the water is frozen.
- ■ Freeze a wet washcloth and let kids play with it straight from the freezer.
- ■ Give toddlers a bowl of crushed ice or snow and some utensils to experiment with.

Bug-Catching Nets

Ages: 2+

Ease of Construction

Description Kids love chasing bugs around with nets, but in all my years working with young children I have never found a net that could stand up to the harsh treatment they dish out. This bug net is proven kid-tough. There are a lot of steps in this project, but none of them is hard. If you can handle a pair of scissors and a needle and thread, you'll do fine.

Learning This is yet another chance for children to get up close and personal with nature so they can practice their observational skills, build a healthy respect for the natural world, and learn about the diversity of life. It also encourages small- and large-muscle development, hand-eye coordination, and logical thinking.

Materials

- ☐ Utility shears
- ☐ ½-inch PEX tubing (a flexible plastic pipe; buy it in the plumbing department of your local home center)
- ☐ Quick-connect union tee (they'll be near the PEX tubing in the plumbing department)
- ☐ ⁷⁄₁₆-inch wooden dowel, 3 feet long
- ☐ Duct tape
- ☐ Friction tape (electrical tape will work too)
- ☐ Netting, about 40 inches square (Mosquito netting works best; you can buy it online if you can't find it locally.)
- ☐ Needle and thread
- ☐ Scissors

Instructions

1. Use the utility sheers to cut two pieces of PEX, one 24 inches long, the other 44 inches long.
2. Attach the shorter piece of PEX to the union tee.
3. Insert the wooden dowel into the same piece of PEX and use the utility shears to trim the dowel to the same length.
4. Wrap the lower 8 inches or so of this piece of PEX with friction tape.
5. Attach the other piece of PEX to the union tee to form a loop.

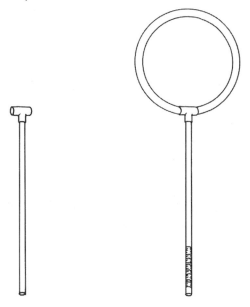

6. Wrap a few layers of duct tape around the point where the union tee and the looped piece of PEX meet.

7. Now, cover the duct tape with a few layers of friction tape. This will complete the handle for the bug net.

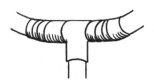

8. Fold the netting in half and stitch the long side together securely.

9. Bunch one of the open ends of the netting together, wrap it securely with thread, and tie it off.

10. Use the needle and thread to stitch the netting to the handle.

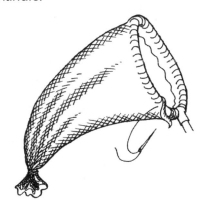

11. Let the children catch bugs. Be sure they release the bugs outside after examining them.

Variations

- Customize bug-catching nets for the kids in your life by selecting their favorite mesh and electrical tape colors.

- Let children use the nets to catch small balls or balled-up socks.

- Encourage older children to draw pictures of the bugs they catch. This is a creative outlet and helps develop their observation skills.

Up Close and Personal

Ages: 2+

Ease of Construction

Description We're going to use magnifying glasses to give children a close-up look at the world and a different perspective on things. They will have fun making their fingers appear bigger, examining their friends' nostrils, and magnifying the words in their favorite books.

Learning Using magnifiers helps children fine-tune their observational skills. They will learn to look for detail and to see more closely. It also introduces them to the usefulness of tools in understanding the world.

Materials

☐ Magnifying glasses
☐ Stuff to look at

Instructions

1. If you like, you can collect some items for the children to look at with the magnifiers. However, it's usually not necessary, because once they see what magnifiers can do, kids will have no problem finding things to look at.

2. Show the children how to handle the magnifiers safely and explain that they make objects appear larger.

3. Send them off to explore. Be nearby to assist and answer questions as needed.

Variations

■ Take the magnifiers outside or on field trips for a closer look at the world.

■ Use your magnifiers to look more closely at the bugs, worms, plants, and other objects discussed in this chapter and throughout the book.

SAFETY NOTE *Supervise this activity closely. Warn children not to look at the sun, and be careful that they don't ignite a fire when around dry materials outside.*

Supporting
Creative Expression and Thinking

The itchy, b****y spider went up the water spout . . .

—words repeatedly sung by a child, nearly 3, in our family child care program

The young singer above had no idea how creative he was being with the song lyrics—he just remembered the words to "The Itsy Bitsy Spider" a bit differently than most of us do. His singing was passionate and full of expression, his hands repeated actions he had learned from his mom and dad, and his eyes sparkled as he sang. And it's true: after being washed out over and over by rain any of us would be a little itchy and probably a little bit "b****y" as well.

We need to do all we can to encourage creative self-expression and thinking in young children so they will grow into adults who are comfortable with these things. In school, there will be plenty of emphasis on memorizing facts and figures. We need to take full advantage of the younger years to stimulate the innate creativity in children. This will serve them well during their school years and throughout their lives.

Our world is always facing challenges that need creative thinkers to develop solutions. It is important for children to practice looking at things with fresh eyes and open minds. Doing so will help them learn that there can be many possible solutions to any given problem. Having a mind full of information is one thing; putting that mind to work creatively using its store of information is something entirely different.

The following activities encourage children to use their imaginations and existing knowledge to think differently and creatively and to express themselves in unique ways.

65

Colorful Magnetic Ice Sculptures

Ages: 3 +

Ease of Construction

Description One way to promote creativity is to provide interesting and unique materials with which children can interact. Magnetic ice cubes fit the bill. When frozen into a hunk of ice, powerful rare-earth magnets will continue to attract and repel each other. Children find the combination of ice and the magnetic field inspiring and are eager to creatively explore the properties of both materials. The sheer newness should keep kids engaged for a long time—or at least until the ice melts!

Learning This project provides a chance for children to work on small-muscle skills, express themselves creatively, learn about cause-and-effect relationships, and deepen their knowledge about the materials.

Materials

- ☐ Plastic containers (Baby food and yogurt containers work well.)
- ☐ Water
- ☐ Food coloring
- ☐ Freezer
- ☐ Small magnets, 2 inches square (We use rare-earth neodymium magnets; they work best. Other magnets *might* work, but these work best.)

Instructions

1. Partially fill your containers with colored water.

2. Place the containers in the freezer until solidly frozen.

3. Add a magnet to each container and top it off with more colored water.

4. Return the containers to the freezer until solidly frozen.

5. Hold the containers under warm water until the ice cubes release.

6. Build an ice sculpture.

Variations

- Use the magnetic ice cubes with the magnetic blocks (see page 67) or other play magnets to broaden the creative options.

- Provide older children with paper clips, silverware, or other metal objects to sculpt with in addition to the magnetic ice cubes.

- Change perspective a bit by building sculptures on a vertical surface like a refrigerator door.

SAFETY NOTE *With good supervision, this activity is appropriate for children three years and up. Keep a close eye on the melting ice so the magnets don't end up in someone's mouth. Children younger than three can also enjoy this activity but, because of the choking hazard, they should be one-on-one with an adult. Bigger ice cubes are better for younger children, who tend to mouth things. Do not allow children to play with loose magnets.*

magnetic wooden Blocks

Ages: 2+

Ease of Construction

Description This set of blocks promotes creativity while offering a safer way for young children to explore the effects of magnets. Magnetic blocks add a whole new dimension to block play. The kids in our program found the resistance they felt while trying to force the similar poles of two magnets together fascinating. Using one magnet to make another one scoot and jump along the tabletop was also a favorite activity.

Learning These blocks offer a great way for children to experiment with the properties of magnets, learn to express themselves with the materials, and increase their awareness of the natural world and physical laws. They will also hone small-muscle skills, hand-eye coordination, and cause-and-effect thinking skills.

Materials

- [ ] 12 to 15 wooden blocks, 1⅜ by 2⅞ inches (We used the domino blocks described in our book *Do-It-Yourself Early Learning*.)
- [ ] ½-inch round countersunk rare-earth magnets (You won't find them many places; we purchased ours online.)
- [ ] ½-inch size 6 flathead Phillips screws
- [ ] Size 6 finish washers
- [ ] Drill and Phillips-head bit

Instructions

1. Carefully insert a screw through the center of one of the magnets and fasten it to a block.

2. Repeat for each magnet. Randomly place the magnets on the blocks. You may also choose to attach more than one magnet to a single block.

3. Screw a finish washer or two to each block so the magnets will have something to stick to. Again, random placement is preferred.

4. Screw a few finish washers to blocks without magnets to add some variety.

5. Show the finished blocks to some children and let them play. Be there to answer questions and intervene, as needed.

Variations

- Use the magnet block set with other magnets.
- Let the children decorate the blocks with markers.
- Hold a magnet block race. Have a pair of children see who can use one magnet block to make a second magnet block scoot across a tabletop the fastest.
- Take the block play from horizontal to vertical on the refrigerator door.

SAFETY NOTE *Don't skip this activity simply because magnets are a part of it. Unlike many store-bought toys that include magnets, these blocks are extremely well made. The magnets are secured with wood screws, so they won't present a hazard for young children. Of course, it's always important to supervise young children at play.*

fun with flashlights

Ages: 1+

Ease of Construction

Description Give children a darkened room and a flashlight and I promise they will quickly become creative. They will draw pictures on the floor and walls with their beams of light. They will become Jedi masters fighting off Darth Vader. They will dance and prance and flit around the room. Flashlights are a tool for seeing in the dark, but they're also tools for creativity.

Learning Children will boost their creativity and imaginations as well as practice their small- and large-motor skills, hand-eye coordination, and visual tracking skills.

Materials

☐ Inexpensive flashlights

☐ Flashlight batteries

Instructions

1. Make sure your flashlights have fresh batteries. There is nothing worse than dead batteries when it's flashlight time.

2. Darken your play area by dimming lights and closing curtains.

3. Give each child a light and some basic rules of engagement. At our house, we keep it simple: no hitting with flashlights and no shining flashlights in people's eyes.

4. Step back, but be there to offer support and assistance as needed.

Variations

■ Secure colored translucent cellophane over the flashlight lens with a rubber band to create colored lights. Your local flower shop or gift basket shop may be able to provide you with suitably sized scraps.

■ Situate a flashlight so it shines a strong beam of light on a nearby wall. Show children how to make hand and foot shadows in the spotlight.

■ Crank up some music, have everyone lie on their back, and create a light show on the ceiling. Pink Floyd or Aerosmith are inspiring.

■ Have children use the light to touch a body part on the opposite side of their body from the hand holding the flashlight. This is an important activity; children who have difficulty crossing their midline (an imaginary line that runs down the center of the body) may have some developmental delays.

Children's Art Gallery Idea

Ages: Infancy +

Ease of Construction

Description Displaying children's artwork is a huge challenge even if you have a big refrigerator and lots of magnets. Kids are usually such prolific drawers, writers, and painters that the projects really pile up. I don't have an answer for dealing with the volume of art, but this project offers a way to properly display it. Both the National Association for the Education of Young Children (NAEYC) and the National Association for Family Child Care (NAFCC) accreditation standards recommend that children's art be displayed at their eye level. We suggest you hang it low, but protect it with a clear piece of acrylic.

Learning When their artwork is displayed, children learn that their work has value. From realizing that, they learn that they, too, are valuable. Also, viewing other children's work stimulates their own creativity.

Materials

- ☐ ⅛-inch clear acrylic panel (Your local home center can cut the stuff to whatever size you want.)
- ☐ Plastic mirror-mounting brackets and screws
- ☐ Drill
- ☐ Tape
- ☐ Children's art

Instructions

1. Determine where you want to create your art gallery and how large it will be.
2. Purchase a clear sheet of acrylic that is sized appropriately for your location.
3. Install the mounting brackets to hold the acrylic panel to the wall.
4. Tape children's artwork to the wall and then install the panel over the artwork. Now the artwork is displayed, but little fingers can't get to it. It won't get ripped down or eaten.
5. To change the display, simply unscrew the panel, put up fresh artwork, and reinstall the panel.

Variations

- ◼ Display other things such as photos of the children, your schedule, or your calendar.
- ◼ Look for possible display spots in your space. We mounted some 8- by 10-inch panels on the Toddler Toy Trough (see pages 82–83) to display pictures of our children's families.

A Cookie Cutter above the Rest

Ages: 2 +

Ease of Construction

Description Simple cookie cutters can be a real creativity booster for young children. Many young artists want to draw lions, hearts, bunnies, or race cars, but their small-muscle skills and hand-eye coordination aren't as advanced as their imaginations. This is where cookie cutters come in—they make great stencils that the children can trace when they're being all artsy and crafty. After tracing the outline, the kids can fill in the detail with paint, markers, or whatever. There is a huge variety of cutters out there to choose from too. We found one Web site that had over seven hundred different cutters.

Learning Tracing a cookie cutter helps develop the hand-eye coordination and small-muscle skills that children need to draw freehand and to write. These skills will also be handy when they decide they want to play the cello like Yo-Yo Ma or the guitar like Jimi Hendrix. This type of activity also helps with visual discrimination, the ability to distinguish visual similarities and differences. Children's creativity is also enhanced by using the cutters to create unique and special pictures to hang all over Grandma and Grandpa's house.

Materials

- ☐ Cookie cutters (Quality metal cutters work best for the not-so-gentle use they will likely receive from young children.)
- ☐ Paper
- ☐ Pencils, markers, or pens

Instructions

1. Demonstrate on a piece of paper how to trace a cookie cutter, fill in detail, and add a background to the picture. Show the kids that they can use multiple cutters to create a unique scene.

2. Let them go to work, but make sure the children have the support and supervision they need.

Variations

- Use the cutters with playdough.
- Trace the cutters with paint to put a new spin on the process.
- Watch as some children inevitably start using cutters shaped like people, vehicles, or animals in tabletop dramatic play.
- Bake cookies! If they turn out, send me some: 1524 Summit Street, Sioux City, IA, 51103.

on a Roll

Ages: Infancy +

Ease of Construction

Description One childhood memory I have of my grandma is how she would put curlers in her hair before bed so she would "be beautiful for Grandpa in the morning." We would sit and talk and I would fiddle with the curlers, handing them to her as she needed them.

Fast-forward thirty-plus years and I'm wandering through a store waiting for ideas for this book to find me when I stumble, literally, into a display of curlers. My mind flashes back to Grandma's house and I decide to take a few packages of them back home to see how the guinea pigs, I mean the children, would use them. They put them in their hair. They used them in block play. They pretended they were cell phones. They carried them around in boxes and purses. They used them in water play. Like the curious and creative children everywhere, they were exploring different ways to use materials that were new to them.

Learning While playing with hair curlers, children will stretch their imaginations and think creatively. This is what they're doing when they take two curlers, hold them together, and look through them like binoculars or when they use curlers as hot dogs in their dramatic play. They will also further develop their small-muscle skills and hand-eye coordination.

Materials

☐ Plastic two-part hair curlers (a variety of sizes and colors)

Instructions

1. Add the curlers to your play environment for the children to discover.
2. Be available to field questions and intervene, if needed.

Variations

■ Introduce the curlers in your block area and show kids how to use them as columns to support other blocks.

■ Use the curlers as rolling pins when playing with playdough.

■ Set them out in your dramatic play area. We've seen children use them as casts for broken fingers when they are playing hospital. One-year-olds like to put them on their toes.

■ Let children roll the curlers through paint to create interesting patterns and textures.

Aluminum foil follies

Ages: 2+

Ease of Construction

Description I thought about including a project that involved creating sculptures out of gold, silver, platinum, or bronze, but I figured those metals just might be budget breakers. So I decided to go with aluminum foil instead. It's cheap, it comes in rolls, and most people know where to shop for more when they run out. Aluminum foil sculptures are more appropriate than those precious metals for another reason—no smelting. Even if you had the budget for gold sculptures, heating them up to 1,064 degrees Celsius might be a bit dangerous with a group of preschoolers. Besides, they would have all kinds of questions I don't want to field: "Is it hot yet?" "Can I taste it?" "Why is the kitchen on fire?" We'll stick with aluminum foil.

Learning Children will practice thinking in new and creative ways. They will improve their small-muscle skills. They will better understand the properties of the material. The will also learn to say the word *aluminum*.

Materials

☐ Heavy-duty aluminum foil

Instructions

1. Wad up some foil and sculpt something yourself to show the children. If you don't know what to make, make an animal. If it has long ears, it's a rabbit. If it has a long neck, it's a giraffe. If it has a hump, it's a camel. If it has short legs, it's an alligator. The point is, you don't have to be a great artist; you just have to give it a try.

2. Let the kids craft their own sculptures.

3. Be there to support them, as needed.

Variations

- Design and build aluminum foil boats. Then see if they float.

- How about making airplanes out of aluminum foil and seeing whose creation gets the most hang time when launched across the yard?

- Wrap things like building blocks or baby dolls in aluminum foil to give them a neat new look.

- Encourage multimedia sculptures by adding materials such as craft sticks, ribbon, and pipe cleaners to your sculptors' studio.

Say Cheese!

Ages: 2 +

Ease of Construction

Description Most kids love hamming it up for photos, but just as many love taking pictures as well. Years ago this activity meant handing disposable cameras to kids and letting them take pictures, but now that the cost of digital cameras has gone down considerably, you may want to consider going digital. Point-and-shoot digital cameras designed for children cost as little as twenty dollars. If you still want to shoot on film, disposable cameras are the way to go, but I suggest going digital.

Learning Children might start learning about photo composition, lighting, framing their shots, and things like that, but mostly they will be taking pictures of their thumbs or their friend's nose. That's what kids do. They will learn to see detail better, they will learn to take turns and share, they will get to practice being careful with the camera, and they will learn to see things with fresh eyes. The camera will become a tool for looking at the world with a slightly different perspective. Using a camera may also enhance their small-muscle skills.

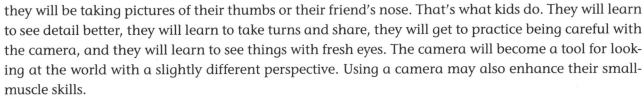

Materials

☐ Inexpensive digital camera or disposable camera

Instructions

1. Show the children how to use the camera. Give them some basic rules for its use and let them know the consequences for not following those rules.

2. Let them take pictures while you remain nearby to offer support, as needed.

3. Print some of their pictures for display.

Variations

■ Vicki Harris, one of my professional mentors, would strangle me if I didn't suggest this: scrapbook the children's photos.

■ Let the children use the camera to document events and activities.

■ Make each child a special CD with pictures to help with remembering your time together.

A Sew-Sew Activity

Ages: 3+

Ease of Construction

Description This is a chance for children to be creative—and maybe poke themselves in the finger with a needle. There was a time when most young girls learned to sew at their mother's side. That doesn't happen as much nowadays, but learning to stitch is still valuable for young girls and boys.

Learning Sewing offers children a new way to express themselves creatively. They will learn to think visually and to be careful with needles. They will learn they can be trusted to use "adult" tools. They will develop their small-muscle skills, fine-tune their hand-eye coordination, develop self-confidence, improve their vocabulary, and develop their thinking skills. This is a good activity for tactile learners.

Materials

☐ Felt pieces, about 4 by 6 inches

☐ Sewing needles

☐ Thread

☐ Scissors

Instructions

1. Demonstrate how to thread a needle and how to stitch the edges of two pieces of felt together.

2. Provide some basic safety instructions.

3. Let the children try their hand at stitching.

4. Be available to answer questions and help out, as needed.

Variations

■ Make sure children who show special interest or skill have an opportunity to challenge themselves with more detailed designs. While test driving this project one little girl used four pieces of felt to sew herself a hat. With some practice, schoolagers may be able to use their new sewing skills to make one of the fabric books described in chapter 1.

■ Challenge children to write their name in stitches.

■ Follow children's lead. Support their interests and see where their new skills take them—they may want to learn to sew on a button or use a pattern to sew a shirt or a superhero cape.

SAFETY NOTE *Some people will hesitate to do this activity because they fear the children may poke themselves with needles. They will. And then they will learn that it hurts, and they'll avoid doing it again. When we were shooting the pictures for this book, a four-year-old boy came up to me and said, "I tried poking myself with the needle to see how it feels. I only tried it five times because it hurt. I'm not going to do it anymore." THAT is real learning. Letting kids work with such small items really is a great way to help them develop motor skills.*

Tilting Towers of Toothpicks and Mini Marshmallows

Ages: 3+

Ease of Construction

Description The idea is simple: give children some marshmallows and toothpicks and see what kind of creative structure they can build. The ends of the toothpicks are stuck into the marshmallows to create shapes and structures.

Learning There is potential for lots of learning here. The activity challenges children's imaginations and creativity. It also encourages problem solving, language development, visual thinking, small-muscle development, spatial reasoning, hand-eye coordination, and premath skills.

Materials

- ☐ Mini marshmallows
- ☐ Toothpicks

Instructions

1. Show children how to build by sticking toothpicks into the marshmallows.

2. Stand back and let them create.

3. Be available to answer questions and assist, as needed.

Variations

- Instead of marshmallows, try gumdrops, grapes, mushrooms, small pieces of potato, playdough, clay, or other similar items.

- Place two plastic bowls on the table about a foot apart. Challenge the children to use their materials to build a bridge from one bowl to the other. Test different bridge designs to see which can hold the most weight.

- Who can build the tallest tower?

- Challenge the children to write their names or ages using the materials.

- Try building three-dimensional shapes such as cubes, pyramids, or prisms.

Dancing in the Dark

Ages: Infancy +

Ease of Construction

Description Glow sticks are another interesting item children can use to express themselves creatively. Simply dim the lights, turn on some music, and let the fun begin.

Learning Shaking their tail feathers while they are shaking their glow sticks not only encourages children to think and move creatively, it works small- and large-muscle groups and develops coordination. Children will also get a good cardio workout.

Materials

☐ Glow sticks

☐ Music

Instructions

1. Create some darkness.

2. Turn up some music.

3. Hand out glow sticks and dance, dance, dance.

Variations

■ Check out the Internet for glow earrings, glow eye-glasses, glow cups, glow hair clips, and other fun stuff.

■ Check out the glow-in-the-dark powder available at www.stevespanglerscience.com. We add it to sensory tubes—the kids love it.

■ Use dancing in the dark as another opportunity to encourage children to cross their midline (see Fun with Flashlights on page 68 for more information).

ZOË SAYS

What would you say if I told you I used to have glow-in-the-dark eyes? Well, I used to think I did. I would tell people that I could see in the dark even when there was no light at all. Like, if my parents and I would be walking down the stairs with the stairwell light off, my mom would tell me to be careful so I wouldn't fall, and I'd say I could see fine because I had glow-in-the-dark eyes.

Sometimes my dad and I would go for walks in the dark so I could use my magic eyes. He would tell me to walk in front of him so he could see where he was going. Kids think all kinds of weird stuff when they are little, but they outgrow it . . . usually.

Bread-Dough Sculpting

Ages: 2 +

Ease of Construction

Description Here is another chance to put the kitchen to work in promoting early learning. Just take ready-made bread dough and give it to children to knead, shape, and sculpt before baking. When the bread comes out of the oven, they can eat their creations along with some peanut butter and a glass of milk.

Learning Manipulating, shaping, and fiddling with bread dough gives kids a chance to use their creativity as well as tune up their small-muscle skills. This activity is good for children who are tactile learners because in addition to sight, they use their senses of touch, smell, and taste.

Materials

- ☐ Ready-made bread dough
- ☐ Cookie sheet
- ☐ Flour
- ☐ Butter or cooking spray
- ☐ Oven

Instructions

1. Make sure everyone washes their hands well.
2. Give each child a hunk of dough to get creative with.
3. Have some flour available in case the dough is a bit too sticky.
4. Grease the cookie sheet and warm the oven.
5. Bake the dough.
6. Let the bread cool.
7. Sample the creations.

Variations

- ■ Provide raisins, cinnamon, chocolate chips, herbs, or other edible bits to mix into the dough.
- ■ Challenge older kids to write their name, make letters and numbers, or create a self-portrait with the dough.
- ■ Forget about baking the dough and just use it as playdough.
- ■ Add a bit of food coloring to the dough.

Taking It Apart

Ages: 3+

Ease of Construction

Description I remember being around six years old and sitting in our dimly lit basement taking apart an old radio. I pulled vacuum tubes, unscrewed knobs, snipped wires, and celebrated a small internal victory every time I was able to remove another piece. I haven't outgrown the impulse. Last weekend I tossed two dump truck loads of stuff out a third-story window because I'm gutting my attic to prepare for a remodeling project for which I have no plans or budget. I just like to take stuff apart.

Kids like to take things apart too. A few weeks ago, I heard Noah, age 3, yell from our bathroom, "Jeff, there's water coming out!"—words no child care provider or parent wants to hear, especially shouted from the bathroom. I went to investigate and was happy to find he'd started unscrewing the toilet's water supply line. There was water spraying all over the walls and floor, but at least it was *clean* water. I quickly tightened the supply line as Noah vowed, "I won't touch that again, okay Jeff?"

To prevent children from taking your toilet apart, dismantling your radio, or gutting your attic, I suggest you find some alternative objects they can take apart.

Learning Taking something apart helps you learn how to put it together and what makes it work. The deconstruction process teaches logical thinking, problem solving, and physics, and it encourages creativity. It's also a prime opportunity for developing spatial awareness, building small-muscle skills, and improving hand-eye coordination. Children may actually learn too much from this activity. A few months after the toilet episode, Noah's mom came in and told us she'd had to hide all the screwdrivers in their house because Noah was taking apart all his toys. His dad had to put them back together, but he did it with a proud fatherly smile on his face.

Materials

- ☐ Things to take apart (VCR, dolls, toy trucks, toasters, radios, stuffed animals, pianos, bikes)
- ☐ Tools such as screwdrivers, scissors, and pliers (This list will vary depending on what the kids are taking apart.)

Instructions

1. Create a safe work area in a somewhat quiet location so little minds can focus without distraction.
2. Choose a child or pair of children to take part in the project and help them get started with the deconstruction. Explain the sometimes-subtle difference between taking something apart and breaking it.
3. Stay nearby to help, as needed.

Variations

- ■ Save parts from things you take apart and use them to create new machines or sculptures.
- ■ Discuss what different components are and how they work.
- ■ Try putting things back together after they've been taken apart.

SAFETY NOTE For safety, snip the cord off any electronics before the demolition begins. Don't ever let kids take apart old televisions or computer monitors.

Developing
Social Skills and Relationships

I love you, Jeff.

—Maddie, almost 4, on her last day in our care

Jeffie, you be Little Red Riding Hood.

—Phoebe, age 2

We began caring for Maddie when she was about eight weeks old and she was in our care until the day before her fourth birthday, when her family moved out of town. While in our care, she learned social and relationship skills that she will use throughout her life. It takes a lot of observation and practice to learn to share, take turns, empathize with others, navigate sticky social situations, read body language, and carry on successful relationships. Our program, along with a great Mommy and Daddy, set Maddie on the right course in her early years, but her social skills will continue to develop and evolve and grow. All of our time together—our conversations, games, dramatic play, cuddling, and long walks—was a chance for her to practice her social and relationship skills. It also made us very close; I love her too.

Phoebe kind of replaced Maddie in our program; she, like Maddie, is an energetic, curious, happy, and engaging child. She and I set right to work getting to know each other and practicing our social skills when she joined our program a few months after Maddie moved away. We played Little Red Riding Hood, we practiced sharing and taking turns, we expressed emotions, and we grew close. Someday Phoebe will move on too. She will leave with some valuable interpersonal skills, and a piece of my heart.

Early childhood learning is not just about small-muscle development and color recognition, although those things are certainly important. Teaching the really important life skills—skills that often determine whether a person finds happiness in life or not—means attending to social and relationship development. Ask a parent what they ultimately want for their child. More often than not, growing a good, kind, and happy person is number one on that wish list. Yet social skills do not come easy; just like anything else worthwhile in life, they require time and hard work. The hours and days you spend interacting with children contribute to their development. Make them count.

Here are some words about social play from Jane Davidson, one really smart person:

> With the great pressure that early childhood programs put on adults to be accountable for what they teach and to cover a certain amount of information, it is easy to see why dramatic play, which appears "fun," will be put aside by the teacher who has many seemingly more urgent demands.

> Although pretend play may look insignificant to the casual observer, there is enormous learning occurring—learning that can be expanded when the adult provides appropriate props, space, time, and guidance.

Jane Davidson, *Emergent Literacy and Dramatic Play in Early Education*

The following pages introduce some simple props and materials to help expand and promote dramatic play. Make sure you provide the needed space and guidance and lots of time. The only way for a child to internalize social skills is through observation and practice, both of which take huge amounts of time. Another thing, remember that children are always watching you. Like it or not, you are their role model for social interactions and relationships.

You've Got Mail

Ages: 3+

Ease of Construction

Description With ever-present e-mail, cell phones, and instant messaging, sending letters through the mail may sound quaint, but this is a great way to encourage social relationships and other learning. Besides, kids will find the whole process fun and exciting.

Learning Children will learn how the postal service works, develop communication skills, build social skills, improve their language skills, and build relationships. Even three-year-olds write well (although adults may have trouble reading it at times). This activity empowers children as writers and refines their small-muscle development.

Materials

☐ Paper

☐ Pens, pencils, or markers

☐ Envelopes

☐ Stamps

Instructions

1. Explain to the children that they are going to write and mail letters to each other.

2. Have each child write a letter and seal it in an envelope.

3. Using home addresses, help the children address their envelopes.

4. Let them stick stamps on their envelopes.

5. Drop the envelopes in the mail.

6. Wait.

7. Celebrate when the mail arrives and read the letters.

Variations

■ Send letters to parents, grandparents, and other friends.

■ Find pen pals to exchange letters with.

■ Teach the children to write and send thank-you letters.

Toddler Toy Trough

Ages: Infancy to 3

Ease of Construction

Description Here is a great way to make toys accessible to young children and give them something to hold on to while they are learning to walk. Infants and toddlers love to crawl in, on, and around our toy trough. We keep it stocked with their favorite toys so there is always something exciting to reach for. The older toddlers like it, too, but we kick them out when they turn three.

Learning The toy trough has become a hub of social activity in our playroom. The children are building relationships, developing language skills, and improving muscle and thinking skills.

Materials

- ☐ Primer and paint
- ☐ Two ¾-inch hardwood panels, 12 inches high by 15 inches wide (end panels)
- ☐ One ¾-inch cabinet-grade plywood panel, 13 inches wide by 4 feet long (bottom)
- ☐ Two ¾-inch cabinet-grade plywood panels, 12 inches high by 4 feet long (side panels)
- ☐ Two hardwood panels, 12½ inches wide by 9 inches high (divider panels)
- ☐ Ruler and pencil
- ☐ 1½-inch wood screws
- ☐ ½-inch wood screws
- ☐ Wood glue
- ☐ Drill with ⅛-inch bit and Phillips-head bit
- ☐ Indoor-outdoor carpet, 4 feet wide by 6½ feet long
- ☐ Finish washers

Instructions

1. Prime and paint the end panels.

2. Make a mark 1 inch in from the bottom sides of each end panel.

3. Secure an end panel to the bottom by lining up the 13-inch side of the bottom between the two marks you made in step 2. Use 1½-inch wood screws and glue to secure the panels. Drilling pilot holes is recommended.

4. Secure the other end panel to the bottom, as described in step 3.

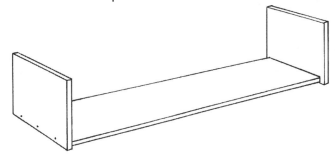

5. Install the side panels using wood glue and 1½-inch screws. The end panels should protrude ¼ inch beyond the side panels.

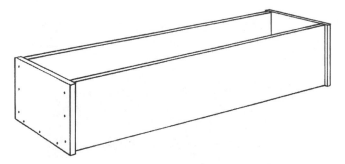

6. You've created the toy trough carcass. Let it set overnight so the glue can dry.

7. Wrap the inside bottom and side panels with the indoor/outdoor carpet. Use the ½-inch wood screws and finish washers to secure the carpet. It will take some tugging and trimming to get it aligned.

8. Insert the two divider panels into the toy trough to create three toy storage areas. Secure the panels with 1½-inch wood screws and finish washers.

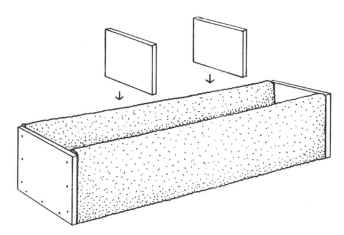

9. Fill the trough with toys and stand back.

Variations

- We secured our toddler toy trough to the playroom floor using 3-inch wood screws. This keeps it in place and allows infants and toddlers to pull themselves up and cruise around.

- Install clear acrylic frames (described on page 69) to display family pictures or children's artwork.

- Securely attach an acrylic mirror in the trough. Young children love to look at themselves.

- Install a steering wheel on one of the end panels. You can find them with the outside play structure materials at most home centers.

- Adjust the trough size to fit your space. Ours is about 6 feet long because we have lots of room in our play area.

Put a Lid on It

Ages: 1+

Ease of Construction

Description Shower caps, hairnets, bandanas, and do-rags are inexpensive and will add a new dimension to dramatic play. We've seen little girls carefully tuck their long hair into a shower cap and shout, "I'm a cowboy," in a deep voice as they swagger across the room. Other children wear hairnets when they're playing restaurant and cover their faces with bandanas when they need to be ghosts. These props are also great for peekaboo with infants and toddlers.

Learning The kids will incorporate these items into their dramatic play and in doing so will build social skills and relationships. They will also refine their small-muscle skills and develop self-care skills.

Materials

☐ Assorted shower caps, hairnets, bandanas, and do-rags

Instructions

1. Add the assorted headgear to your play area.

2. Be available to answer questions, assist, and intervene as needed.

Variations

■ Add other hats and headgear to your dramatic play area. Make sure to rotate items every few weeks to keep play fresh and fun.

■ Wear shower caps to play in the sprinkler.

Give Them a Hand... and a foot

Ages: 1+

Ease of Construction

Description Here are some more everyday items that encourage social learning. Adding a selection of socks, gloves, and mittens to your dress-up clothes deepens children's dramatic play experience. The children at our house will put on gloves and mittens and pretend to have snowball fights in the middle of July. They have also been known to put on three or four pairs of socks, wear mittens on their feet, and use socks as bags to haul small toys around the house.

Learning All of the above weirdness involving socks and gloves encourages conversations, sharing, taking turns, social problem solving, small- and large-muscle skills, hand-eye coordination, and creative thinking. Children are also learning life skills while pulling the socks and mittens on and off. This activity also encourages children to cross their midlines, an important skill in brain and physical development.

Materials

☐ An assortment of socks, gloves, and mittens

Instructions

1. Introduce the materials to your play area.
2. Step back and let play and learning happen.
3. Be available to answer questions and help, as needed.

Variations

- Wear gloves or mittens during water play or while painting.

- Play a game of What's in the Sock? Stick a small toy or household item into a sock and ask the children to guess what is inside by feeling the outside of the sock.

- Have dressing races. See who can put on a pair of socks and a pair of gloves quickest (grab those wristwatches from chapter 2). Another option for older kids is to have them put a pair of socks on their hands—and then race to see who can put on and button a shirt fastest.

It's a wrap

Ages: 2 +

Ease of Construction

Description The kids in our program love to pretend to be doctors or veterinarians. They wrap baby dolls and stuffed animals up like mummies and tend to each other's broken arms and legs. Elastic bandages are a great prop to encourage this type of pretending. These simple objects are a wonderful spark for lots of creative play.

Learning Children learn social, nurturing, empathy, and caregiving skills while bandaging stuffed puppies or baby dolls. They will also improve their language skills, small- and large-muscle skills, and hand-eye coordination.

Materials

☐ Elastic bandages

Instructions

1. Show children how to use the bandages, and give them some rules for appropriate play. The bandages should never be wrapped too tightly or placed around someone's neck.

2. Step back and let them play. Be available to help or intervene, if needed.

Variations

■ Attach one end of a bandage to the ceiling and secure a stuffed animal or doll to the other end. Then let the brave toy do some bungee jumping.

■ Outside, secure a bandage between two tree limbs to create a big slingshot. Grab the bungee-jumping toy from the previous variation and see how far it flies.

■ Use a bandage to wrap older children's legs together for three-legged races.

■ Secure two older children's arms together and challenge them to complete tasks like tying their shoes or putting on socks.

Phoebe's two-year-old eyes sparkled as she scanned our playroom, taking in her new child care environment. The room was full of things for her to contemplate and manipulate, clatter and scatter, riddle and fiddle—and she did. From the very beginning, Phoebe was comfortable with the equipment in our play area, but it took some time for her to feel at ease with the people. Within a few days, though, she'd learned everyone's name and stopped referring to the other children as "that guy." She began engaging in more parallel and group play as she grew more comfortable with the environment and the other children. When there was a disagreement over a toy, she used her words. She relaxed and got to know everyone better. Our routine quickly became her routine.

We were getting in tune with each other. She even seemed to notice my energy waning each day around late morning, because she started giving me a nap between 10:30 and 11:00. "Jeffie, lie down," she would command as she tugged at my hand. She had a pillow and a blanket waiting across the room. I would dutifully lie down as she handed me a doll or stuffed animal to cuddle. Then she covered me with all the blankets she could find, gently reminding me to go to sleep if I dared to raise my head.

As we grew better acquainted, she more frequently incorporated me into her play. Not only did I get naps, but I was offered food and drink when she played restaurant, given gifts (toys wrapped in doll blankets) when she played birthday, attacked by imaginary owls when she went hunting for owls, left feeding her baby when she had to go to work. Phoebe grew to feel at home in our care, comfortable, relaxed, happy, eager to learn, trusting, and engaged. Knowing that we would keep her safe and healthy, she was now free to play, explore, and discover the world as it existed in our playroom.

Building this trust—making children like Phoebe feel safe, comfortable, and at ease enough to take learning risks—is the most important, and the most difficult, part of caregiving. Young children are constantly confronting the unknown as they discover the world for themselves. Children need encouragement to face the unknown— and a safe haven they can retreat to when they need to recharge. We have to build safe emotional environments. We have to simultaneously hold them close and support their drive to explore the world.

A Clean Sweep

Ages: 2+

Ease of Construction

Description For children, the line between work and play is very blurry—and so is the line between toys and work tools. Kids will play with anything. Brooms and dustpans pass the Empty Box Test with flying colors. Children like to pretend to be grown up and do adult work. Besides, they make most of the messes; they might as well help clean them up!

Learning The dramatic play that brooms and dustpans stimulate will help kids learn valuable self-care skills, improve their social skills, help them learn responsibility, improve their small- and large-muscle skills, and fine-tune their hand-eye coordination.

Materials

- [ ] Child-sized brooms and dustpans (or some regular ones downsized)

Instructions

1. Show children how to sweep and use the dustpan.
2. Give them some basic rules for appropriate use of the materials.
3. Let them play, but be available to help or intervene if needed.

Variations

- Use a small ball and some brooms for a game of broom hockey.
- Put the kids to work sweeping up after meals and activities.
- If necessary, make messes for the kids to sweep up. Try using shredded paper or scraps from craft projects.
- Designate some brooms and dustpans for outdoor play.

Stick to It

Ages: 1+

Ease of Construction

Description Children have been playing with sticks of all sizes in our yard for many years. They use them as walking sticks when they are hiking through the bushes on bear hunts. They pile them up and pretend to build a fire and roast marshmallows when they play that they are camping. They use them to poke holes in the ground. They drag them, pull them, tote them, stack them, roll them, and line them up on the ground. They do not throw them, use them as weapons, or poke people with them.

Number of stick-related injuries we have had: zero.

Learning Sticks will encourage dramatic play, which gives children a chance to practice social skills and build relationships. They will also practice following rules, build small- and large-muscle skills, hone hand-eye coordination, and improve language skills.

Materials

☐ Sticks

Instructions

1. Build a collection of sticks.

2. Develop some ground rules for safe play as well as consequences for not following those rules.

3. Make children aware of the rules.

4. Let them play.

5. Be available to support their play and enforce your rules, as needed.

SAFETY NOTE *It's always important to keep a close watch when youngsters are at play. This activity is no exception.*

Variations

■ Introduce sticks of different sizes. We have some that are over 15 feet long and 6 inches in diameter. It takes a lot of cooperation and communication to haul these things around the yard.

■ How about playing with branches? A few years ago I was pruning some shrubs while the kids played in the yard. They asked if they could play with the pile of branches I had trimmed. They used them to build a "tree house," planted them in the sandbox, built a wall around the sandbox, and hauled them from one side of the yard to the other.

■ Let them decorate some sticks with paint.

■ Challenge them to use sticks to write their names in the sand or to form the letters of their names.

A Brush with Greatness

Ages: 1+

Ease of Construction

Description Adding some inexpensive hairbrushes and combs to your dramatic play area will encourage social play and promote other learning. The kids at our house love to use these adult "tools" to play beauty shop or barber.

Learning The children will learn social skills and build relationships when they incorporate hairbrushes into their dramatic play. They will also develop life skills and improve small-muscle skills.

Materials

☐ Hairbrushes and combs

Instructions

1. Add a few brushes and combs to your play area.

2. Be available to assist and intervene, as needed.

Variations

■ Try using hairbrushes and combs as paintbrushes.

■ Have children use their fingers to draw letters on the bristle side of a brush. This is a great activity for tactile learners because it helps them literally get a feel for the letters.

■ Try gently running a soft-bristled brush on the arms and legs of an infant or toddler. This can help with sensory integration and is also a good therapeutic activity for children with sensory integration disorder.

mirror, mirror, on the wall

Ages: Infancy +

Ease of Construction

Description Children of all ages enjoy looking at themselves in the mirror. They like to make faces, twirl their hair, give themselves kisses, and admire their good looks. The problem with most mirrors is that they're not mounted at child height, which makes it challenging for kids to see themselves. We fixed this problem and it makes using mirrors much easier.

Learning The saying "know thyself" has been attributed to a number of dead Greek guys, but it is good advice—and being able to see yourself is part of knowing yourself. Children will learn to express themselves, study their body language, practice pouting and smiling, and maybe learn to wink while playing in front of a mirror.

Materials

- ☐ ⅛-inch acrylic mirror, sized to your space
- ☐ Mirror mounting brackets
- ☐ Drill and bits

Instructions

1. Find a good location for your mirror. You want to mount it as low to the floor as possible so that even infants on their tummies will be able to watch themselves.

2. Use the mounting brackets and tools to attach the mirror to the wall. The process will vary, depending on your wall type.

3. Let children discover the mirror; then watch them watch themselves.

Variations

- ■ Small hand mirrors can be fun and promote lots of social play, but make sure the mirrors are acrylic or shatterproof to avoid injuries.

- ■ Challenge older kids to write letters backward so they will look correct when held up to the mirror.

- ■ Challenge them to make different faces in the mirror. See if they can do happy, sad, shy, angry, and excited.

cardboard cylinders of Learning

Ages: Infancy +

Ease of Construction

Description Okay, it's another fancy name for something pretty simple. What we're talking about here is the cardboard container that oatmeal comes in. In our program, the infants fiddle with them and roll them around, the crawlers push them and chase them, the toddlers use them to haul things around the house, the two-year-olds stack them to make towers, and the older children like to punch out the bottoms and stick them on their arms and legs as either casts or big muscles.

Learning All the play I mentioned above leads to the development of language skills, social skills, small- and large-muscle skills, thinking skills, and a deeper understanding of the physical world. These containers are full of heart-healthy goodness when you buy them, and they are full of learning opportunities when the oatmeal is gone.

Materials

☐ Empty oatmeal containers

Instructions

1. Introduce a few of the containers to your play area.

2. Make sure you are available to support and build on the children's play.

Variations

■ Cut a container in half lengthwise. The halves can be used either as tunnels for small cars or as cradles for baby dolls.

■ Decorate the containers and play them as drums.

■ Get more empty containers by baking oatmeal raisin cookies. (If you have any extras, you know where to send them.)

Going, Going, Gone

Ages: 1+

Ease of Construction

Description The first thing my wife, Tasha, said when I completed the original ice-cream bucket potty was, "What if they really use it?" My answer was that we would throw it away, clean up, and eat a few gallons of ice cream so we could make another one.

It's been years since we added this prop to our play and we have never had a child try to use it for real. The kids, stuffed animals, dolls, cars, and puppets all pretend to use it. They even drop small blocks into the bucket sometimes to represent . . . well, use your imagination.

This is the perfect social-play toy for young children, because so much of their time and conversation revolves around the potty. They are either going, getting ready to go, being asked if they need to go, or being cleaned up after going someplace they were not supposed to go.

They will love and play with this project because they can relate to it so closely. Besides, they know they are not supposed to play in the real potty and this is the next best thing.

Learning The learning that comes with this project is social; children will deepen their knowledge of proper potty protocols and social etiquette and they will converse and laugh and joke about potty-related topics. They will also practice some of the physical skills needed when using the potty and they will bathe in rich language.

Materials

- ☐ Cardboard box, approximately 4 inches by 8 inches by 15 inches (potty tank)
- ☐ Newspaper
- ☐ Duct tape
- ☐ Round plastic 1-gallon ice-cream container (potty base)
- ☐ Round plate, plastic lid, or bowl, 5 to 6 inches across (to be used as a template for the potty seat)
- ☐ Two lids from round plastic ice-cream containers (potty seat and potty lid)
- ☐ Marker
- ☐ Utility or craft knife

Instructions

1. Pack the cardboard box with crumpled newspaper and tape it shut. This will make it a bit stronger and help it hold up a little better.

2. Remove the handle from the ice-cream container.

3. Securely tape the ice-cream container to the cardboard box.

4. Center the plate on one of the ice-cream container lids and trace it.

5. Use the knife to cut out the circle you made in step 4. This lid will become the seat of your potty.

6. Use the knife to cut the lip off the other lid so you end up with a flat round piece of plastic. This will be the potty cover.

7. Use duct tape to create a hinge and attach the lid to the seat.

8. Secure the seat and lid to the potty base—just snap it onto the bucket. Make sure your duct tape hinge aligns with the cardboard box so the lid opens correctly.

Variations

- We used an old-fashioned clothespin and some wire to create a flusher for our potty.

- One of the children put the potty in a wagon and pulled it around. He told us he had made it into a port-a-potty.

Lights, Camera, Action

Ages: 1+

Ease of Construction

Description Take a few minutes to add this pretend video camera to your play props and the kids will all be screaming for their close-ups in no time. They will pretend to make movies and they will integrate the video camera into their imaginary outings. It's an easy way to add a new dimension to dramatic play.

Learning This is a social play booster that will lead to conversations, discussions, and probably even an argument or two. This is good, because the best way to learn to interact appropriately with other people is to practice during play. When children play out situations with this prop, they will be learning how to deal with similar situations in real life.

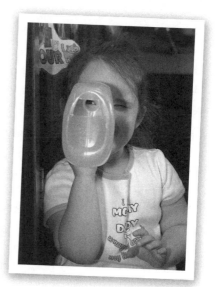

Materials

☐ Plastic juice or syrup container (one with a handle), empty and clean

☐ Utility or craft knife

Instructions

1. Remove and discard the container's lid.

2. Cut a hole, approximately 1 inch square, in the bottom of the container. Make sure the hole is opposite the opening in the top of the container, so you can look in one hole and see out the other.

3. Show children how to look through the container and pretend it is a video camera. Send them off to play.

Variations

■ Hot-glue a few milk jug lids to the side to serve as camera knobs and buttons.

■ Have a few children act out a scene for another child to videotape.

■ Ask children to make videos of special events like birthdays or a child's first steps.

Can You Hear Me Now?

Ages: 2+

Ease of Construction

Description A few years back Hunter, age four at the time, asked me if he could borrow "those ear things" I wear when I mow my lawn. His mom had just gotten tickets to see the monster trucks and he remembered how loud they'd been the previous year. He'd spent most of the evening with his hands over his ears; that made it tough to eat popcorn and enjoy the show. He knew that my "ear things" would free up his hands. I lent them to him. They worked so well that a year later when the monster trucks rumbled back into town, Hunter borrowed the earplugs again.

Those "ear things" have also proven to be fun during play. A child puts them on and tries to hear her friends. Then the friends talk louder, or yell, or pretend to yell. Sometimes a child puts on the earplugs and sits and gazes out the window for a long time, then says, "I just needed some silence in my head." Other times kids pull them on and off their ears as fast as possible to enjoy the weird sound effects.

Learning Children learn to appreciate their own hearing, empathize with people who have limited or no hearing, and learn to be better listeners. We have noticed that the earplugs also encourage children to be more aware of body language and that they often look for other ways to communicate, such as by writing or using hand signals.

Materials

☐ Earplugs or earmuffs (headsets)

 *Use the kind of earplugs that sit on top of the ears, not the little buds that slip into the ear.*

Instructions

1. Add the earplugs to your play area and let the children discover them.

2. Be available to support their play, as needed.

Variations

■ Let the children experiment with another type of sensory deprivation by using a bandana to cover their eyes.

■ Challenge them to create their own sign language or help them learn some American Sign Language (ASL).

■ Ask older children to write about what it would be like to lose their hearing or another one of their senses.

Building
Physical Skills

As soon as crawlers crawl and toddlers toddle, they start to make messes. They dump, they pour, they knock over, they strew, they toss. These are all basic physical skills taken for granted by adults but essential to cooking, planting crops, construction, and many popular team games. Coordination requires endless practice.

—Elizabeth Jones and Renatta Cooper, *Playing to Get Smart*

I was in a hurry to play!

—Hunter, age 5, explaining why he peed on our front sidewalk instead of in the bathroom

We began caring for Hunter when he was about six weeks old, and he was enrolled in our program until he outgrew us. In our care, he learned to roll over, sit, stand, toddle, walk, talk, shout, whisper, jump, cut, scribble, doodle, write, hop, skip, gallop, march, run, toss, throw, hit, climb on chairs, climb stairs, climb on tables, and climb trees. By the time he left us at age six, he even learned to confine most of his peeing to the bathroom.

Building the large- and small-muscle skills needed to do all those things is a huge task that starts at birth and goes on for years and years. Children need lots of opportunities to develop and practice these skills. They need chances to repeat the same actions over and over and over again until they are mastered. Then they need to be encouraged to move on to the next physical challenge.

Children also need to practice using their senses. Previous activities in this book have emphasized various senses and there are more to follow. These activities will help children develop the ability to differentiate and discriminate among different things by using their senses.

Just how do you provide opportunities to develop physical skills? It's easier than you might think. Opportunities for physical development and learning are all around us in our everyday environment. Children work on small-muscle skills by doing things like coloring, handling small objects, ripping paper, clapping, driving toy cars, and picking their noses (although there are probably more sanitary small-muscle activities they could engage in). Large-muscle skills get a workout from doing virtually anything that involves those muscles—swinging, walking up and down stairs, playing games of tag or hopscotch. When you begin thinking about how the children in your care move their bodies throughout the day, it becomes easy to incorporate activities into your routine that stimulate physical development.

Shredded

Ages: Infancy +

Ease of Construction

Description Shredded paper is a great manipulative for tiny and curious hands. We've used it in small quantities and we've dumped garbage bags full of the stuff on the floor for the kids to frolic in. I remember my buddy Kia, not yet two, burying herself in a pile of paper shreds so all I could see was her big brown eyes and huge smile. Then she growled and burst from her hiding place like a wild animal. After the attack, she burrowed back into the pile to await another opportunity to pounce on a passing victim.

Learning Playing with paper shreds will work large- and small-muscle groups. It will also encourage creativity, build language skills, and improve coordination.

Tip: If you don't own a paper shredder, ask office workers you know to save some of this by-product for you.

Materials

☐ Shredded paper

Instructions

1. Dump some shredded paper in a sensory table or on the floor.

2. Be available to support play and assist, as needed.

Variations

■ Use shredded paper in water play.

■ Moisten some shredded paper, freeze it, and let the children explore it.

■ Use it in the sandbox or while making mud pies.

A Real Swinging Time

Ages: Infancy +

Ease of Construction

Description On one of the many hooks in our playroom ceiling, we often hang a rope for the children to play with. While we don't have enough space for the kids to swing from it, they have fun playing catch. They also use it as a pendulum and try to knock things over. Infants will sit on the floor and shake it. Toddlers hold on to it and walk in circles. After a while, we simply unhook the rope or tie it up and move on to another activity.

Learning Children will build small- and large-muscle strength and control. They will also improve their hand-eye coordination, logical thinking skills, understanding of the physical world, and social competence.

Materials

☐ Anchor and eyebolt

☐ Soft nylon rope, at least 1 inch in diameter and long enough to reach from your floor to the ceiling

☐ Carabiner clasp

☐ Scissors

☐ Threaded hook

☐ Drill and bits

Instructions

1. Secure the eyebolt to your ceiling. The methods for doing this will vary depending on the type of ceiling you have. The eyebolt needs to be firmly attached.

2. Securely tie the rope to the carabiner clasp.

3. Attach the carabiner clasp to the eyebolt.

4. Tie a large knot in the bottom of the rope and cut the rope so it hangs a few inches off the floor.

5. Stay close as the children explore the swinging rope.

6. Attach the hook high on a wall so the loose end of the rope can be hung over it when the rope is not in use.

Variations

■ Tie a stuffed animal, small pillow, or soft doll to the rope and let the children play catch.

■ Add another eyebolt to the ceiling and tie a second rope between the two eyebolts. Attach the first rope's carabiner to this rope. Let the kids pull the hanging rope back and forth on the ceiling rope, kind of like a dog chain attached to a clothesline.

■ Attach a cowbell to the carabiner to add a new and noisier dimension to the play.

■ Hang a rope from the ceiling that the children can actually swing from. In her book *Together We're Better,* Bev Bos shows how to do this.

SAFETY NOTE *Some readers may be having heart palpitations thinking about young children playing with a rope. That's understandable, because a rope and a group of unsupervised children <u>could</u> result in a serious injury. In a supervised environment, however, this is just another prop to enhance learning and play.*

Terrific Times with Tape

Ages: Infancy +

Ease of Construction

Description Zoë loved tape when she was little. When she was about four we gave her dozens and dozens of rolls of different kinds of tape as a Christmas present. She opened the package and smiled—then quickly headed off to play. She made dolls into mummies, she built things, she fixed things, she decorated herself. She learned.

Learning The biggest thing our daughter learned while manipulating duct tape, transparent tape, packing tape, masking tape, and electrical tape was small-muscle skills. She has great dexterity. Through this play, she also grew creatively, learned to problem solve, learned about cause-and-effect relationships, learned about physics, and expressed herself artistically.

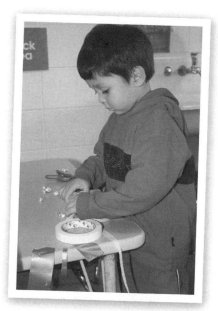

Materials

☐ Tape, assorted kinds

Instructions

1. Set some ground rules.

2. Give the tape to the children and let them explore.

3. Be available to answer questions and intervene, as needed.

Variations

- Bunch up wads of tape, sticky side out, for infants and toddlers to explore.

- Make tape available during arts and crafts.

- Use painter's tape to make numbers and letters on the floors or walls. It is less sticky and easier to remove.

- We sometimes put strips of masking tape down on a tabletop just so the toddlers can pull it up. It is good for developing the muscles in their fingers that they'll be using when they learn to write.

ZOË SAYS

When I was a kid, my favorite toy was . . . ready for it? TAPE. Yep, tape. I used to tape blocks and boxes together to make furniture for my Barbie dolls or give them broken limbs by taping up their arms and legs. A couple of times, I taped boxes together to make boats.

Build a Very Versatile Sensory Station

Ages: 1+

Ease of Construction

Description Although making this sensory table involves a few power tools and more steps than most of the projects in this book, the results are well worth the effort. The tote simply lifts off the base and can be replaced with another in seconds. This means you can keep a few totes around full of sensory play items—rice, oatmeal, wood chips, and similar things—and just pop them onto the base when you want to use them. Kids will still make messes during sensory play, but your setup and cleanup times will be drastically reduced. Thanks to Debby Bullis, a family child care provider in South Dakota, who created the original version of this table.

Learning This sensory station will help develop small-muscle strength and coordination. Its use will also promote language acquisition, logical thinking, problem solving, hand-eye coordination, environmental awareness, and creativity.

Materials

- ☐ 1-inch PVC pipe, two 10-foot sections
- ☐ 1-inch PVC 90-degree elbows, four
- ☐ 1-inch PVC tee fitting, six
- ☐ 28-quart plastic totes, 22.9 by 16.8 by 5.9 inches
- ☐ ¾-inch size 10 pan-head sheet metal screws, four
- ☐ Saw or pipe cutter
- ☐ Cordless drill

Instructions

Note: To make this project using a different size tote, simply adjust the length of the bottom rail pieces. The other measurements should work fine for most totes.

1. Cut the pipe lengths as follows:

20-inch piece, three (top rails and stretcher)

12-inch piece, four (upper legs)

8-inch piece, four (lower legs)

7¼-inch piece, four (bottom rails)

2. To make a leg, use a tee fitting to connect an upper leg piece with a lower leg piece. Make four legs in this manner.

3. To complete the leg assemblies, attach a bottom rail piece to the open tee-fitting hole in each leg.

4. To build the stretcher assembly, attach a tee fitting to each end of the 20-inch stretcher.

5. Connect the leg assemblies to the stretcher assembly.

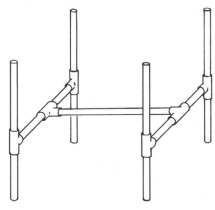

6. Attach 90-degree elbows to the ends of the two 20-inch top rails.

7. Install screws in the elbows leaving approximately ⅜ inch extending from the elbow.

8. Attach the rail assemblies from step 6 to the top of the base.

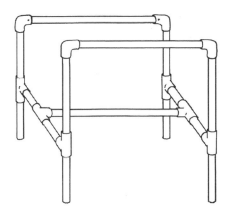

9. Press pieces together firmly to make sure all connections are secure.

10. Set a tote in place so that its outer rim rests on the screws.

11. Add fun sensory items and let the children play.

Variations

- Use the sensory station outside during messy play.

- Remove the lower legs to make the sensory station toddler height.

- Experiment with odd combinations of materials that will engage multiple senses. For example, try oatmeal and mud, birdseed and water, leaves and plastic dinosaurs, or chilled watermelon and cantaloupe rinds.

- In her version, Debby attached two adjustable luggage straps between the top rails. This is a great option for supporting the tote without having to install screws.

ZOË SAYS

Let's face it, kids are messy. *When you give them stuff like a tote of oatmeal or rice to play with they are going to get it all over the place. Lots of adults don't let kids play with things like this because of the mess and that is a problem. Little kids need to play with this stuff. They will make a mess, but they are practicing using their senses and developing their muscles—that is important stuff.*

I've always been messy and probably always will be. When I was a kid, I had a playroom and you could barely ever see the floor. Nowadays you can barely ever see the floor in my bedroom. It bugs my mom because she's a little clean-freakish. The thing with me having a messy room is I can usually find what I'm looking for. The fun thing is that when I'm looking for one something, I might find something else I thought I'd never see again. It's like getting an unexpected present!

what's That Smell?

Ages: 2+

Ease of Construction

Description Of all the senses, the sense of smell is the one that we tend to neglect developing during early childhood. With this activity, kids close their eyes, sniff different items, and guess what they are smelling. Simple, easy, fun.

Learning Children will learn to differentiate and discriminate between different scents. Children need opportunities to develop and hone their senses and practice using them. We tend to take the senses for granted, but children need time and opportunity to learn to use and understand them.

Materials

☐ Small containers with lids, empty and clean (Baby food or yogurt containers work great.)

☐ Smelly stuff, such as onions, cinnamon, peppermint, ketchup, and oranges

Instructions

1. Stick small amounts of each item in individual containers and put lids on them.

2. Have the children close their eyes.

3. Uncover a random container and give each child a chance to sniff its contents.

4. Ask the children to guess which item they smelled.

5. Repeat with each container.

Variations

- Chart the results of their sniffing. How many kids were able to guess every item correctly? Which item did the most children guess correctly? Which one did the fewest sniffers get right?

- Close your eyes and let the children pick items for you to smell.

- For younger children, skip having them close their eyes and just let them smell the different items.

- Try putting two items in a container and see if kids can guess what both of them are.

Totally Tubular

Ages: 1+

Ease of Construction

Description Years ago we attached a heavy-duty cardboard tube, like the ones carpet comes on, to the underside of one of our playroom tables. One end is attached to the underside of the table and the other end touches the floor. The kids love sending cars, bouncy balls, and other objects down the tube. One of the first things infants do when they start walking is head for the tube with a car, for they've been watching older children do this for almost their whole lives.

Learning Children will build small-muscle strength and control while stuffing toys down the tube. They will also learn about gravity, the laws of motion, and cause-and-effect relationships.

Materials

☐ Heavy cardboard tube

☐ Handsaw

☐ Drill

☐ 1½-inch wood screw

☐ Washers

☐ Duct tape

Instructions

1. First, find your cardboard tube. Home centers or flooring stores will probably be happy to give you one.

2. Figure out where you will install the tube, hold it in place, and use the handsaw to cut it to size if it's too long.

3. Secure your tube in place. We mounted ours by first installing a wood screw and washer from the inside of the tube, through the cardboard, and into the underside of the wooden table. To secure the lower end of the tube, we installed another screw and washer through the tube and into the bottom of the rail that runs between the legs on the other end of the table. To firm it up a bit we used some duct tape around the stretcher that runs the length of the table. You may have to modify this installation based on your particular table and tube.

Variations

■ Instead of a cardboard tube, use a section of 4-inch PVC pipe.

■ With some plastic anchors, some wood screws, a drill, and some know-how, you can install the tube on a wall instead of under a table.

■ Our kids like to lay plastic racetrack at the low end of the tube. Then the cars they drop in the top of the tube zip out the bottom end and along the track.

■ Try sliding things up the tube. We use blocks. We just add them one at a time until the tube is full. Then the fun begins: they start falling out the other end and crashing to the floor.

Streamer Balls

Ages: Infancy +

Ease of Construction

Description After I gave a talk about do-it-yourself learning materials a few years back, a provider suggested a variation to the streamer launchers (see page 30) I had shown the group. She thought that instead of attaching the flagging tape to a rubber band, I should hook the tape to a bouncy ball. I made myself a note and as soon as I walked into the house, I borrowed a bouncy ball from Zoë and built a prototype.

We tried it out with the kids the next day and they loved it. My favorite streamer ball game is Go Get It, which I particularly like to play with toddlers. I toss the ball; they retrieve it. I toss it again; they retrieve it. This goes on until one of us gets tired. We used to call this game Fetch, but we changed the name so as not to offend any parents. It's still the same game, though, and it really is cute when the kids crawl across the floor with the streamer ball in their teeth and drop it at my feet. I always make sure to scratch them behind the ears before I toss it again.

Learning Children learn small- and large-muscle control and develop strength in those muscles as well. They also increase their language skills, hand-eye coordination, and understanding about the physical world.

Materials

- ☐ Flagging tape
- ☐ Scissors
- ☐ Finish washers
- ☐ 1-inch wood screws
- ☐ Marker
- ☐ Drill
- ☐ 2-inch bouncy balls

Instructions

1. Cut three or four lengths of flagging tape between 2 and 4 feet long.

2. Stack these pieces together. Fold them in half lengthwise to find their center, and mark it.

3. Place a finish washer on a screw and then use the drill to screw through the flagging tape (where you marked it) and into the ball.

4. Give it a bounce and then make some more.

Variations

- We have made balls with very long streamers and very short streamers. You can also vary the number of streamers you attach. This all affects their weight and how they fly through the air.

- Use different colors of flagging tape.

- Cut four pieces of flagging tape about 3 feet long. Stack them together and make a knot in the middle. Now, attach a ball to each end. Give it a toss.

- Encourage children to toss and catch with their nondominant hand.

I hate sitting still. I've never been able to, and I never will. When I was little I was always busy and my mom thought I never slept. Maybe if I'd had a few streamer balls back then I would have been so tired from running around that I would have slept more.

Nowadays, kids are told to sit still too much. Like how in school the kids have to sit almost all day. Then, when they do get to get up and play outside during recess, they're not allowed to play tag and there's a designated area to run in. Little kids need to move to learn.

The Hole

Ages: 1+

Ease of Construction

Description In her book *Teaching By Heart*, Mimi Brodsky Chenfeld describes visiting a child care center in California that had a large hole the children loved to play and learn in. We gave it a try in our yard and it has led to hours of play, exploration, and learning for kids of all ages. It's really quite simple: they dig, get messy, make discoveries, exercise, and have fun. Modern children don't have nearly enough dirt under their fingernails and this is a great remedy.

Learning Children will build small and large muscles, improve their coordination, learn about the physical world, use all their senses, problem solve, improve their language skills, practice social skills, and learn about blisters.

Materials

- ☐ A place to dig
- ☐ Shovels, scoops, and spoons
- ☐ Buckets and other containers

Instructions

1. Make sure all underground utilities are marked and the area you want to let the children dig in is safe. Call your local utility company or 811 to get your utilities marked for free.

2. Set some ground rules about where kids can dig and what they can do with the dirt.

3. Dig a few scoops yourself to show the kids how it's done.

4. Let them dig.

5. Be available to help and intervene, as needed.

Variations

- Just add water. A muddy hole is full of messy fun!
- Look for treasure and discuss what kids find.
- If your hole doesn't produce its own artifacts, bury treasure for the kids to find.
- Add dump trucks, tractors, and other vehicles.

outside Play Talking Tube

Ages: 1+

Ease of Construction

Description The PVC pipe used to make this project will carry children's voices—even the softest whispers—from one side of your outside play area to the other. Children will integrate the talking tube into their play. It will become a telephone, the speaker at a restaurant drive-up window, a machine for talking to aliens, or a microphone for them to sing into.

Learning This project will promote language and social development as well as stimulate imaginative dramatic play while the children scramble from one side of the play area to the other. It will also help them hone their hearing and voice control as they talk to each other through the tube.

Materials

- ☐ 90-degree 1-inch PVC street elbows, six
- ☐ 1-inch PVC pipe, two 10-foot pieces
- ☐ 1-inch PVC connector
- ☐ 1-inch pipe strap, four
- ☐ ¾-inch galvanized or stainless steel screws
- ☐ Drill and Phillips-head bit
- ☐ A wooden fence to mount your talking tube to

Instructions

1. Attach three of the street elbows together, as illustrated.

2. Attach the other three street elbows to create a mirror image of the assembly from step 1. These assemblies will be where the kids talk and listen. This design will help prevent them from stuffing things like sticks and sand into the talking tube.

3. Connect the two sections of long pipe with the connector, and mount them to the fence using two of the pipe straps and some screws. You may choose to use more or less pipe to better fit your play area. Install a pipe strap near the middle of each pipe section. Make sure you mount the pipe at a comfortable height for the children.

4. Attach the assemblies from steps 1 and 2 to the ends of the pipe and secure them with pipe straps.

5. Let the children play.

Variations

- Use other pipe fittings to add extensions so the kids can talk from multiple locations.

- To hook your talking tube to a chain-link fence use zip ties.

■ Install the talking tube underground if you don't have a fence to attach it to. First, call 811 to have underground utilities marked. Then dig a trench about 12 inches deep for your pipe sections. Attach a 90-degree elbow to each end. Then install a 4-foot section of pipe to each elbow so it extends vertically out of the trench. Install the assemblies from steps 1 and 2 on the upper end of the 4-foot pipes. Fill in the trench. Now, pound in a steel fence post next to each of the 4-foot risers and secure it to the riser with cable ties.

Hefting and Hauling

Ages: 1+

Ease of Construction

Description I'll never forget the afternoon, way back in my child care center director days, when an old guy came to the door and invited me out to his pickup truck to see if we could use what he wanted to donate. My eyes lit up when I saw that he had five or six large trash bags filled with pinecones. He told me that when his kids were small, they would heft and haul pinecones all over their acreage. They filled wagons and wheelbarrows and bushel baskets and old pillowcases. They stacked them, smashed them, mixed them with water and mud to make soup, and tossed them around. He told me the darn things got to be a nuisance back then, but now that his kids were long grown and gone, he hated to see the pinecones just lying there.

With his help, I dumped out a few of the trash bags in one corner of the center's playground and got out of the way. Within minutes kids were filling pails and trucks with the pinecones and hauling them around the playground. The old guy smiled and said he'd be back in a year with more pinecones.

Learning When children do all this hefting and hauling, it leads to stronger, better coordinated small- and large-muscle groups. It also encourages creativity, social skills, language development, problem solving, spatial reasoning, and premath skills.

Materials

☐ Items to haul, such as pinecones, bricks, sticks, rocks, pea gravel, dried leaves, mulch, logs, or cement pavers (Heavier items encourage cooperation and build strong muscles.)

☐ Baskets, buckets, small wheelbarrows, and bags to haul things in

Instructions

1. Make the materials available and step back so play can begin.

2. Be available for support, as needed.

Variations

■ Create opportunities for indoor hefting and hauling by using blocks and manipulatives such as stuffed animals, pillows, toy cars, or books.

■ Give the kids a real-world challenge by having them help arrange chairs and carry dishes at mealtime, or maybe by taking out the trash.

■ Decorate all those pinecones, rocks, and bricks with paint or markers.

Tie one on

Ages: 1+

Ease of Construction

Description Kids get to practice tying, lacing, buckling, Velcro-ing, or zipping with this project— it's a bunch of shoes mounted on a board. We mounted ours on the back of a toy shelf. The kids sit and fiddle with the laces and buckles. It's hilarious when they try to keep their balance with one foot on the floor and the other in a shoe they're trying to tie. Talk about building physical skills.

Learning Children will learn important self-care skills as well as improve their hand-eye coordination and small muscle skills.

Materials

- ☐ ¾-inch plywood panel, 12 inches wide by 24 inches long
- ☐ Three or four old shoes with laces, buckles, zippers, or Velcro straps
- ☐ Wood screws
- ☐ Drill and bits

Instructions

1. Screw the shoes to the plywood panel. Make sure there are no sharp screw points sticking out anywhere.

2. Mount the wooden panel to a wall or cabinet at child height.

3. Let the children test their skills.

Variations

- ▪ To keep things fresh, change the shoes on the panel every so often.

- ▪ Knot shoe laces into the first set of eyelets to help prevent them from being totally removed from the shoes.

fun in a Pinch

Ages: Infancy +

Ease of Construction

Description Wooden clothespins provide a great way to develop the small muscles of the hand. It doesn't really matter how kids use them. I have seen children hang pretend laundry, clip clothespins onto the edge of a cardboard box, attach them to their hair while playing beauty shop, hang them from their lips, and cover their backs with them so they can become porcupines.

Learning Children will strengthen small muscles in their hands and improve their dexterity. They will also increase their creativity, problem-solving skills, language skills, social skills, and thinking skills.

Materials

☐ Wooden clothespins, nonhinged

Instructions

1. Set out a bunch of clothespins in your play area.

2. Support children's play and be available, as needed.

Variations

■ Hang a child-height clothesline in your play area and provide some clothes for the children to hang.

■ Clip some clothespins on an infant's clothes and watch the child tug and pull at the strange objects.

■ Let the children decorate the clothespins with markers.

■ Encourage kids to cross the midline and use their nondominant hand when playing with clothespins. For example, clip clothespins to the children's left shoes and challenge them to use their right hands to remove the clothespins.

ZOË SAYS

As I was holding vibrant and curious Marygrace the other day she decided to drop the toy she was holding. I know it was an intentional act because of the way she looked at me before holding it out to her side, releasing it, and tracking it to the inevitable clunk on the floor. She wanted to play the how-many-times-can-I-make-you-bend-over-and-get-my-toy game; I'm sure you've played. To adults, it can be an exasperating game; to infants and toddlers, it's learning.

While adults tend to categorize learning, dividing it into topics and subtopics, children are busy learning everything at once. Someday little Marygrace will decide where she wants to focus her learning—perhaps on subatomic chaos theory or noneuclidean geometry— but for now she simply wants me to bend over and pick up that fascinating little loop with the primary-colored beads. At this point in her development she wants to learn as much as possible about as much as possible. Young children learn incredibly fast and they tend to blur the lines between our adult categories. In fact, all at once this simple drop-the-bead game is teaching Marygrace a bit about language and literacy, math and logical thinking, science and problem solving, creative expression and thinking, social skills and relationships, and physical skills. Talk about exhausting!

Air Launchers

Ages: 2+

Ease of Construction

Description This one was all Noah's idea. Age two at the time, he was busy fiddling with toys in our toddler toy trough one day when he put half a pink plastic egg on top of an empty chocolate syrup container. Then he gave the container a quick squeeze and the plastic eggshell flew into the air. Noah's eyes bugged out of his cute little head and he did it again, then again—then about three thousand more times. Other kids scrambled to find appropriate containers and eggs so they could try it. Soon it was raining pastel plastic eggs.

This activity is so simple and so fun, and I am so jealous that I didn't think of it myself.

Learning This activity is a good way to hone small-muscle skills, but it also promotes logical thinking, problem solving, creative thinking, language skills, and social skills. Oh, and large-muscle skills, too, because once you send your egg into the air, you have to hunt it down before you can send it sailing again.

Materials

☐ Plastic chocolate syrup, dish soap, or maple syrup container with a squeeze top, empty and clean

☐ Half a plastic egg

Instructions

1. Make sure the spout on your container is fully open.

2. Place the egg half on top of the container.

3. Give the container a quick and forceful squeeze. The air blasting from the container will send the piece of plastic sailing.

4. Demonstrate for the kids and let them play.

5. Be available to support them, as needed.

Variations

■ Instead of the egg half, use those paper condiment cups you put ketchup in at fast-food places.

■ Use a hula hoop or laundry basket as a target for your flying egg halves.

■ Experiment. Try a variety of different materials and see which ones work and which ones flop.

A fun Catcher Dealy-Bopper

Ages: 2+

Ease of Construction

Description Kids will love building and then challenging themselves with this easy-to-make catching game. It's nothing more than a plastic container taped to a paint stick, but it will offer lots of fun and excitement.

Learning This little apparatus will help develop hand-eye coordination as well as large- and small-muscle skills and coordination.

Materials

- ☐ Paint stir stick
- ☐ Plastic yogurt or similar-sized container, empty and clean
- ☐ Duct tape
- ☐ Aluminum foil

Instructions

1. Make the catcher by taping the container to one end of the paint stir stick. Make a few of them.

2. Wad up pieces of aluminum foil to make some small balls.

3. To play, have one person toss a foil ball while someone else tries to catch it.

Variations

- ■ See how far apart you can stand and still catch the balls.
- ■ Let each child try to catch ten tosses. Record the results and chart how many tosses each person catches.
- ■ Experiment with different-sized containers, balls, and sticks.

Pig Puzzle Template

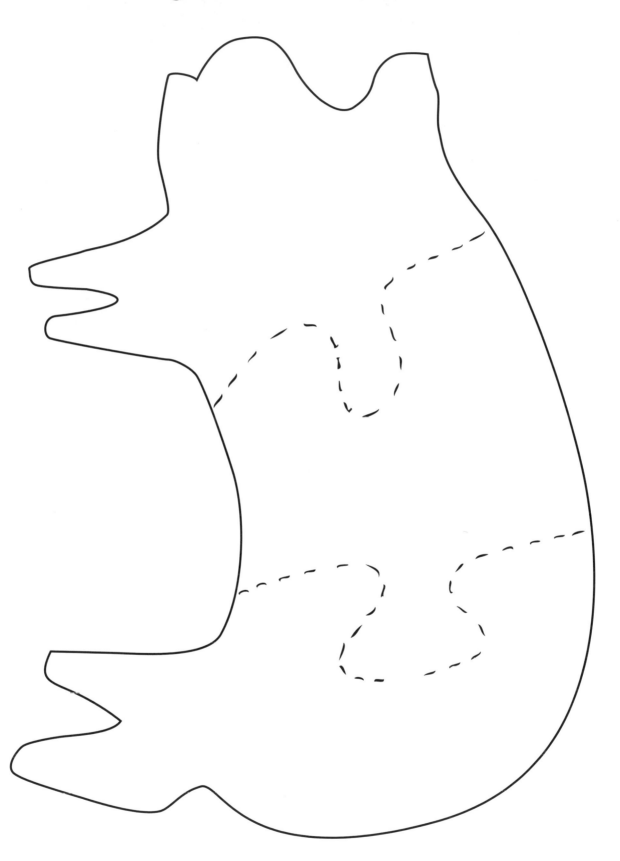

Turtle Puzzle Template

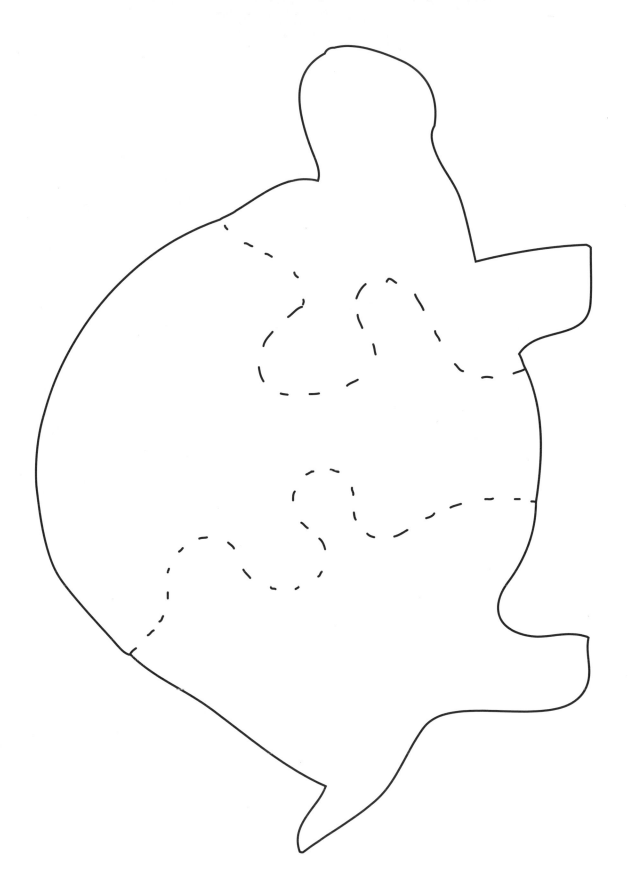

Duck Puzzle Template

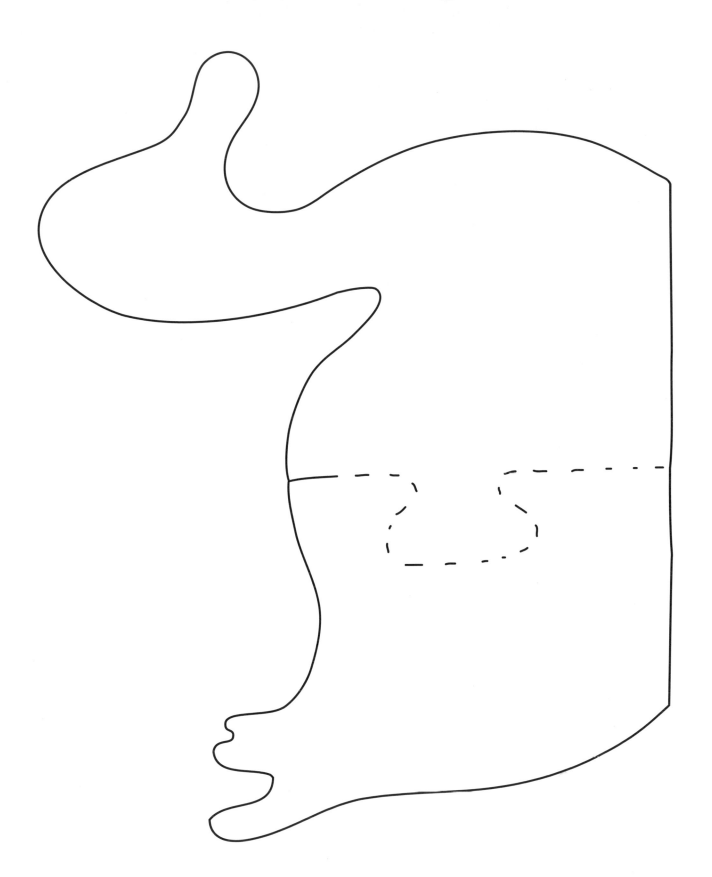